THE PEOPLE'S GHOST STORIES

COMPILED
BY
RICHARD FELIX

If you have
any ghost stories please
email them to

ghost@richardfelix.co.uk

or visit
richardfelix.co.uk

This Book is
dedicated to

The late
Mr. Harry Martindale

The man who told
the best ghost story in the world

First published in Great Britain in 2020
by
Felix - Lilley

All rights reserved. No part of this publication may be reproduced, stored in any retrieval system, or transmitted in any form, or by any means including electronic, mechanical, photocopying, recording or otherwise without the prior written permission of the copyright holders, nor be otherwise circulated in any form or binding or cover than in which it is published and without a similar condition being imposed on the subsequent publisher.

The author and publisher have made every effort to contact the copyright holders of the pictures in this book.

Apologies are made to anyone who has been missed.

I would like to thank all that have sent their ghost stories for inclusion in this book

Thank You
Richard x

Foreword, from the editor Richard Felix

Having lived with ghost stories from the age of four and being frightened of ghosts since that age, due mainly to those stories told to me by older children who then sent me back home with a dread of the oncoming night and all the terrors that it held for me alone in my bed. I thought it was time that I compiled a book of ghost stories. A different book of ghost stories. Stories straight from the horse's mouth. Not stories handed down from generation to generation that often turn into Chinese Whispers. Not stories gleaned from hours of research in libraries or trolled from the internet. Not stories penned by writers with creative or imaginative minds. Not stories from professors, Parapsychologists or supposed experts in the paranormal field. But stories from you, "Joe Public". First- hand accounts from those who have experienced Ghosts, whatever Ghosts are!

Over the past twenty-eight years I have conducted Ghost walks in Derby, York, Chester, Chesterfield, Leicester, Bolton and Ashbourne. I have been involved in TV programmes including Most Haunted, Great British Ghosts, The Scariest places on Earth, The Y Files and Ghost Detectives. Created forty-one Videos of haunted counties in Great Britain and written eleven books on the subject.

Wherever my ghost hunting travels take me, I interview, talk to and listen to, people who have witnessed the paranormal.

I personally have seen a ghost, heard a ghost, travelled with a ghost, and been touched by a ghost. Do I consider myself an expert on ghosts? No, how can anyone be an expert on something when there is no proof of its existence?

I do believe that in some form we do exist after death. I believe that the word ghost should be substituted for the word Energy.

One of the most powerful arguments supporting the concept of life after death are the laws of nature. The most basic law is the first law of thermodynamics, which states that energy can neither be created nor destroyed. Its form can be changed by physical or chemical processes, but its essence can never be altered.

The human mind is made of electromagnetic energy and since energy can't be destroyed the mind cannot cease to exist. There is a possibility that the human mind exists separately to the brain. Hence reports of human transplants bringing with them thoughts and memories from the dead donor.

If the mind does function separately to the body, when the body dies the mind will continue to exist independently from the body. The mind, the awareness of your personality, consciousness, ego, soul, spirit, YOU, will continue after material death.

All this is hypothetical, no proof exists, yet! It must be labelled speculation, fantasy, imagination, and spiritual insight. "Nothing to do with science, no proof". Yet... hang on a bit... nothing we can dream of, no matter how unbelievable, can come anywhere close to the spectacular designs of the universe and beyond, which we know so little about.

In 1986 Voyager 2 sent incredible photos back to earth of one of Uranus's moons called Miranda.

The photos revealed dramatic landscapes, golden mountains with huge fountains of molten metal shooting thousands of meters in the air. These images transmitted back to earth revealed scenes more fantastic than anything we could find in our wildest science fiction films. Voyager uncovered enough startling information to force us to re-examine many of our theories about the solar system.

Recently astrophysicists discovered that about 90% of the Universe is formed from invisible dark matter, allowing us to see only 10% of what is actually out there. It is believed that these invisible particles are passing through our bodies all the time. No one knows what they are or where they come from. There are so many things that we do not know about the universe and beyond. How it originated or what was there before if anything.

Voyager alone uncovered enough new information to make us re-examine our many theories about the solar system lot of scientific texts will have to be re- written to include this new data.

There is a certain amount of scientific data sustaining the idea that our awareness and our personality survives material death. For scientists to make statements about the possibility of life after death without verifiable, unsubstantiated experimentation would be the kiss of death for their name and reputation.

Despite this some scientists are convinced that there is a verifiable argument for the survival of the human mind after death but are hesitant to publish their theories because of the lack of real proof.

So where do I get my proof of life after death from. You, talking to you over the last twenty-eight years. Listening to your ghost stories. No! what I should say is accounts not stories.
Your hundreds and hundreds of accounts over the years have given me all the proof I need.

Over years of listening I have found it easy to differentiate between the truth and fiction. Some people were overtired, drunk, mistaken, making it up but the vast majority genuinely believed what they experienced.

The accounts you are about to read in this, your book, are from ordinary genuine folk who believe what they encountered was real.

You will notice how similar some of the accounts are. They will be from different locations and times. They will never have met but they all have one thing in common. They encountered a ghost.

This book is all the proof needed.

The first ghost story in this book must come from the late Harry Martindale who told what I believe to be the best ghost story in the world. I had the privilege to interview Harry on the spot where this ghost story happened.

Harry was a very brave man to tell his story back in 1953 as ghosts and the supernatural where still being ridiculed. If it was not for people like him, I believe that the ghost industry would have never evolved has it has to this day. Harry sadly died in October 2014.

It was 1953, York, 18-year-old Harry Martindale, a heating engineer was in the cellar of Treasurer's House. Unbeknown to Harry it was a very haunted building. He was in the barrel-vaulted cellar on a small step ladder drilling a hole through the barrel-vaulted ceiling. He was all alone. All of a sudden he heard a trumpet blast, the mind of course has to rationalise what it is hearing, he didn't think to himself, "Oh a Roman trumpet", he just looked down the corridor and thought someone has got their radio on very loud. He then heard the trumpet again but this time he could tell that it was coming from the wall in front of him. As he looked down a Roman soldier started to appear out of the wall and as Harry said to me "What do you do when you are frightened, you step backwards", and of course Harry was on a step ladder. He stepped back and fell off the ladder on to the floor. He sat there amazed as about twenty Roman soldiers, two by two, came through the cellar wall towards him.

He was terrified. His first comments were to himself, "Oh my God they are Roman soldiers what will they do to me?" They did nothing to him, they didn't see him, but he could see them. He described them in great detail. The strange thing was that they were little Roman soldiers, they were no more than four feet high and they had got no legs. He described them in such detail he could tell that they had got stubble on their faces. He described their helmets, the small shields, the little swords and the spears that they had got in their hands. At the back of them a Roman soldier on a horse came through and again he described the horse in great detail. They all passed him without making comment, without looking at him without even noticing he was there and disappeared through the other wall. Harry scrambled to his feet and ran. Halfway up the stairs he bumped into the curator of Treasurer's House who said to him, "You look as if you have seen the Romans." Harry turned to him and said, "Why didn't you tell me?" He left the building, went back to his yard and told them what they could do with Treasurer's House. He never even got his tools back. On the way home he called at his doctors and the doctor put him on the sick for two weeks with stress. Being an eighteen-year-old lad Harry told his mates, everybody laughed at him, everyone ridiculed him until eventually Harry stopped telling the story. Do remember this was 1953. Harry went on to be a York City policeman for thirty years, a credible guy, not one to make up silly ghost stories. In the early 1970's they did an archaeological dig underneath Treasurer's House and eighteen inches below the cellar floor they found the Via Decumana, the old Roman road in the same position where Harry had seen his Romans. Those Roman soldiers had their sandalled feet on the original Roman road, probably made of granite, eighteen inches below the present cellar floor which cut them off at the knee and made them appear legless. Harry is not the only person to see Romans in Treasures House. At least five other people have seen them since 1900, always in February. I believe that what Harry saw on that fateful winter's morning was a recording of a tragic and very traumatic incident involving a Roman Patrol heading back towards the Roman Fort who were ambushed by invading Barbarians at the end of the Roman occupation of Briton.

    I believe that Harry's Romans were nothing more than a holographic recording held in the silica in the granite Roman road. One thing I have not done is to check how damp the cellar is in Treasures House. I use this ghost story on every ghost walk, talk, lecture and after dinner speech that I do.

    Twelve years ago, my youngest son Wills had the opportunity to make a DVD called Ghosts of York. I could not do this without featuring an interview with Harry Martindale. I rang him up and introduced myself and told him what we had planned. He stopped me by saying that he did not talk about the incident at Treasures House anymore as he had recently had serious heart problems after coming out of a lecture that he was doing about ghosts. I quite understood where he was coming from and said to him "Thank you for talking to me it has been a real privilege to talk to you as I use your story on every event that I do and can I just tell you that you are my hero", the phone went silent for a moment and then this voice said "Go on then I'll do it."

He completed the most fantastic interview in the cellar, on the very spot where he saw his ghosts and I asked him at the end of the interview if he believed in ghosts and he said to me, "Only the ones that I have seen". To be honest meeting Harry Martindale was the highlight of my ghost hunting career.

Richard with the late Harry Martindale on the very spot where he saw his Romans.

The next story is from Mr. Stephen Lilley I have known Steve for over 25 years, and he has travelled the world with me filming and producing my ghost DVDs. To say Steve is a ghost sceptic is an understatement. He did not believe at all until!

Dear Richard here is the story I promised to send you for your "Peoples ghost story book" As you know I have been with you when literally thousands of people have told ghost stories to you on the Ghost Tour of Great Britain. I don't believe these people were lying or making things up, but I always put it down to they were mistaken or wanted to believe in something that didn't exist.

As a child my parents and grandparents were deeply religious people, Until the age of 18 I had to go to a Pentecostal church with them three times on a Sunday. Yes very happy clappy speaking in tongues and casting out evil spirits in people! I saw it all! and this is why I probably put up a barrier not to believe in ghosts and the paranormal.

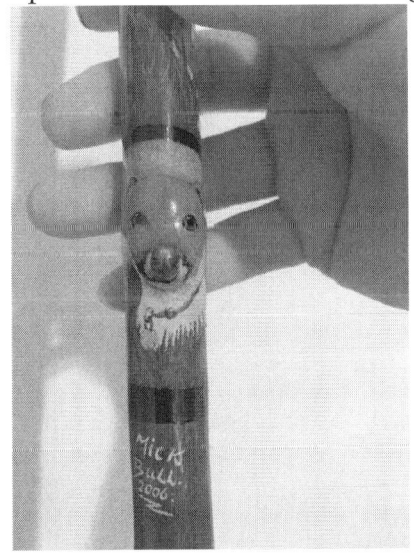

However, this happened to me in 2019 a paranormal experience what cannot be explained.

I had a dog called Dave, he had been my companion and best friend for over 17 years but sadly I had to have him put to sleep in October 2019. Dave was a big part of my life and I had never felt so guilty in having him put to sleep and I was terribly upset!

The day after Dave had died, I woke up in the morning walked down the stairs and a walking stick which had been painted with a portrait of my friend Dave threw itself at me! I do not mean just fell over or something like that, I mean launched itself right across my path and it hit my chest! This walking stick had been propped up against the wall in a corner for over three years since we had moved into this house! And I honestly believe this was Dave saying to me "it's all right mate I'm happy now" I hope he wasn't saying "you had me killed you bastard" However I believe it was the spirit of Dave saying something. This happened! do not understand it, but it happened.

Steve

Dear Richard, I would like to submit a story for you, I hope you find it suitable.

The cat's paw

 I was twelve years old at the time, 1966, and my parents and I lived with my grandparents, that is, my mother's parents. We had a dog; Timmy was his name and not unlike any other dog. He enjoyed company and liked to play and benefited from all the comforts of home. I recall it was a Saturday, about mid-afternoon and my parents and grandparents were sat in the front room watching television. Dad and granddad watching the sport whilst mum and my grandmother chatted over a cup of tea. Being an only child I was quite used to amusing myself and I was charging around the rest of the downstairs with my plastic sword saving the world from dragons, as one does as a child, along with my trusted steed – Timmy; the weather being somewhat inclement outside.

I had just rid the world of my third dragon when I noticed Timmy behaving in a very uncharacteristic fashion. Now, the stairs to the upper floor of our mid terraced house came down into the middle room, the door of which, when opened away from the stairs would then double as the door to the kitchen; the house, it has to be said, was quite old. The door at this time was back against the stairs and secured by a hook and eye to stop the dog from venturing upstairs for crafty nap on one of the beds. This left a three-inch gap between door and the bottom of the stairs. Timmy had taken an interest in something in the well of the stairs and was trotting back and forth pausing only to push his nose into the gap and sniff loudly. He then started to try and force his way through the gap, he pushed and pushed until his feet could no longer keep a firm grip on the floor and the more, he tried, the more agitated he became. Suddenly, he became aggressive, growling and snarling with the hackles on his neck raised and teeth barred with the whites of his eyes clearly visible. It was as if he were trying to attack something on the other side of the door. I thought for a moment that he might pull the fastenings from the woodwork and took a couple of steps back unsure as what to do for I felt that to approach him might give him cause to turn upon me! This behavior lasted for about a minute, although it seemed much longer, when suddenly he stopped. Now he just stood there and looked, just for a few seconds and then he took on a more submissive demeanor. He lay flat to the floor with his ears flat to his head and started to whimper. A couple of times he shuffled on his belly away from the door clearly afraid and I could see that he was shivering quite violently. I called to him to come away from the door, but he took no notice and I called to him several times more, but no notice did he take. Eventually I approached him and gave him a firm tap on the rump with my sword and at this point he slowly backed away but not taking his eyes from the door and his tail firmly tucked between his legs. His mood had changed from that of a dog protecting his territory to that of an animal that was extremely scared. Suddenly, he ran to the back door with a whimper and I straightaway opened it and let him out into the garden – as much for my own safety as for his.

Puzzled and confused by this strange behavior I went to the foot of the stairs and peered through the gap into the darkness beyond. Of course, I could see nothing. I sat there for some time pondering the events of the last few minutes and as I did so, completely involuntarily, I tapped the sword back and forth between the door and the partition that closed off the stairs staring blankly at nothing in particular. I became aware of a resistance, a tugging and it felt as though someone, or something was trying to pull the sword from my hand. Unsure for a moment of what was happening and responsively I tugged back only to find that whatever was on the other end had tightened its grip! I looked down at the sword and because my eyes had become accustomed to the gloom, I saw the paw of a black cat extended through the gap from within the stairs with its claws firmly hooked into the sword. Now I screamed like a girl and ran into the front room frantically trying to tell the family of what had just happened. My father and grandfather both ran up the stairs while I remained with my mother and grandmother at the bottom. The house was searched thoroughly upstairs and down but no evidence of a cat, or any other animal for that matter could be found. Because of the weather no windows in the bedrooms were open to allow the entry or, for that matter exit of any furry intruder. Timmy, my dog, took a lot of persuading to come in from the garden and, he would never venture up those stairs again.

A vivid imagination some might say. However, my grandparents did have a black cat, a cat that would dwell on the stairs because it never liked the dog but it had died some three weeks before these events of which I speak. As for my sword, well, on closer inspection there was not a claw mark to be found! There were no more occurrences such as this ever again but sometimes, Timmy could be seen sniffing at the afore mentioned gap at the bottom of the stairs before hurriedly trotting, tail between his legs to his place of sanctuary under one of the dining chairs; a favourite hiding place of his.

Regards Ron Smith

It only seems to be dogs' cats and horses that see ghosts. And we only seem to see the ghosts of them. One reason may be that they have co-habited with us for at least twenty thousand years. As far as I know no-one has ever reported a haunted abattoir or seen a ghostly badger.

Dogs especially seem to have a sixth sense. They know when someone is about to die or can detect if someone has cancer.

Many years ago, I was talking to a chap who told me that his Alsatian warned him twenty minutes before he was going to have an epileptic attack.

Cats have their own built in satellite navigation system. Drop your cat off in Portsmouth and a week later it will turn up on your doorstep.
I Have two stories to tell. Although I have never seen a ghost, but I certainly have felt and seen what a ghost can do.

1. Back in 2008 I woke up at 2.25am for no apparent reason, however, I had a feeling something was going to happen. I felt, what I can only describe as a 'fluttering' just above my chest. Then I felt an ice-cold hand move up my left arm and stroke my face. When I say ice cold I mean absolutely freezing. I was very scared but at the same time I was hoping this was my nan who I was very close to. My Nan passed away in 1989. About two years after this I went to see a medium. My husband's family took over the whole meeting and I was left feeling a little sad. As I was walking away the medium said it was your nan who touched you. I had said nothing of this and was delighted. My Nan has not visited me since though.

2. My mother in law, Margaret, passed away in August 2017. At the time of her death my husband and his sister fell out and were not speaking. Their argument happened in front of Margaret while she was in her hospital bed, much to my disgust. Anyway, literally a couple of weeks after Margaret passed, I was having a bath. In my bathroom I had a string of gold hearts across the wall. I looked over and the string of hearts was going up and down with two of the hearts being flicked left to right. I wasn't startled. It was a joy to see. I knew instantly it was Margaret's way of asking me to get her son and daughter reconciled. This I did although sadly they have both fallen out again! Margaret has not come back in that way again but I know she is around.
Kind regards
Janice Griffiths, Longbridge, Birmingham. UK.

There is no doubt in my mind that our loved ones are around us, especially in times of trouble.

Here are my ghost stories.

Years ago, I bought a house with my then husband, it was a larger than usual Victorian terrace with three floors. Upon moving in I felt that there was something not quite right, I felt that there was a spirit of a woman attached to the house, but I wasn't concerned about this.

Not long after moving in I used to see her often, usually out of the corner of my eye and I told my then husband. My husband dismissed it as rubbish because he didn't think that ghosts existed. He was soon to change his mind.

I had started a job as a care assistant, and I used to work night shifts, so I slept for the majority of the day. One day I was awoken to my then husband shouting me asking me to come downstairs. I asked him what was wrong, and he told me that he had seen the ghost of a lady.

He told me that he was washing up and had heard footsteps behind him. He thought that it was me and without turning round he told me to go back to bed. The footsteps moved closer towards him and he turned round expecting to see me, instead he saw the ghost of the woman that I had seen on previous occasions.

Needless to say, I didn't have much sympathy and told him that I hope that he believed me now and I went back to bed.

There were several incidents like this, but this is the best one. It's even more credible when your husband sees the ghost as most men poo-poo the idea of ghosts.
Women are more sensitive than men, that's why they see more ghosts.

I have a few ghost stories from my local town and nearby towns.

Years ago, when I left school at the age of 15, I got a job at the local Yates Wine Lodge in my town Ashton Under Lyne. I worked there for many years starting as a pot collector and then moving up to a barmaid and cleaner.

When I started working there, I was warned that the ghost of a lady was quite active there. I paid no heed to it because we had spooks in my house growing up and I was used to this type of thing.

Every night when I was working, I used to go into the back kitchen and turn on the dishwashers and I'd also turn on the one behind the bar.

Every time that I stood in the back kitchen, I could feel someone standing behind me, I'd turn round and there would be no one there. This would happen in the bar area, and the area of the bar that I used to open up to go and collect glasses.

It started to get really intense and I mentioned it to the landlord. He told me that I wasn't the first to complain about this and if it got too much, I could take a break.

She was highly active in the pub and in the derelict building above the pub that used to be the hotel part of the pub. We often saw her shape walking round various areas in the building.

One night as we rang the bell for last orders all the staff and myself were stood together having a rest. We all saw an old blunt knife that we used as an ice pick levitate up in the air, move towards us and fall standing up point down onto the floor. This was impossible to do because the floor was stone.

I picked up the knife, but everyone was spooked by this. Most didn't want to be alone in the bar area.

I was also told of an incident that happened to another employee that worked there. She worked there for many years and instead of going home after the afternoon session she used to go upstairs and have a bath and relax in the old coaching house (hotel) area.

She ran a bath and decided to have a soak. As she was sat in the bath, she saw the spirit of the woman stood right at the side of the bath. Needless to say, she never had another bath there.

There was also another abandoned bar upstairs that was closed to the public. It was a regular occurrence to open up the bar in the morning and find all the glasses smashed on the floor.

From Charlotte Hughes

Dear Richard

I've never believed in ghosts but during my time working in various property's over the years I've seen some odd stuff. The most memorable being when I was working as a boiler installer in Hull.

It was one of those flat roofed late 70s concrete houses, hardly a spooky old mansion. Just typical social housing. We started the job, my colleague removing the boiler in the kitchen and me upstairs replacing the valves on the radiators. The stairs went up to a landing on the right with 2 doors to the bedrooms, no other access up or down.

About an hour into the job I was hunched over on the small stair top, swearing at a rusted valve I couldn't remove, when I felt the weight of a hand on my shoulder and someone squeeze past. This didn't raise an eyebrow as I presumed it was my colleague carrying out his work, so I leaned to one side to let him pass onto the small landing.

At this precise point I heard my colleague shout from the kitchen 'somebody just went upstairs!'. I sat up and was confused. The resident was at work; my colleague was downstairs, so who had passed me towards the bedrooms?

Fearing it was the rogue scrap collectors that had been plaguing the jobs stealing materials; I jumped up and checked both bedrooms. There was no one there. I went back to the landing where my colleague was standing halfway up the stairs asking 'who was it?'.

I told him that someone had pushed past me, and I thought it was him and he said he had DEFINITELY seen someone in a black coat go upstairs. We both stood looking puzzled.

We checked the doors front and back, they were locked then we checked upstairs again, there was no one.
With no explanation and a wage to earn we carried on with the job. Upon her return we informed the resident about the strange incident.

She was neither shocked nor disturbed as apparently a figure was regularly seen in the property along with unexplained noises

As I said, I've seen and heard strange stuff before, but never actually had a sighting and physical contact together.

Andy Peacock.

Dear Richard,

I grew up in a mining village in Nottinghamshire, and my family home was one of the Pit cottages, actually a terrace of six elevated large houses, built for the men who 'sank the pit'. My mother was born in the house and lived there for the most ninety-five years. She had never moved but her address actually changed when the council was renumbering, and New Row became Main Street.

At each end of the terrace were steps and an entry that took you round to the rear of the properties. Another interesting and significant feature in this case was that if you lifted the floor boards you could shine a light from one end to the other, which also meant that although we didn't really hear our neighbours, we could hear people using the entries and steps.

This story happens before I was born. The old lady next door had been very poorly and was in her last hours, her husband, a miner, had died some years before. When he worked shifts at the pit, he would walk up the steps when he arrived home and kick the wall three times as he walked up the entry.

My dad and my grandparents were sitting in our house and my mum and another neighbour were on death watch next door, sitting with the old lady in her final hours.

Suddenly they all heard, from their respective places, someone come up the steps from the street, walk with heavy boots up the entry, kick three times on the wall, and then walk to the door where the footsteps stopped. At that moment, the old lady took her last breath......her husband had come to fetch her.

Both households were startled by what they had heard, and both couldn't believe what they had heard, but agreed that he came to fetch her at the time of her death.

Many nurses have told me over the years, that they know when a patient is about to die as a dead relative comes to get them.

From Elaine Loydall

Dear Richard,

Our house has always had strange things occur...whether it be doors opening and closing, lights and taps go on by themselves, or toys stuck to the ceiling, only to drop as soon as you enter the room,

We have caught multiple pictures of what we believe to be the young spirit, whom multiple eye witnesses have seen, a young girl, maybe ten or eleven, wearing a white dress with a blue sash, she is often heard giggling, and is seen most frequently on top of the stairs of our house.

Our house belonged to the Lutterels, the original owners of Dunster Castle. It was a maid's quarters, then an orphanage, a hotel, and now our family home for the past 16 years.

Attached are two images, the first of my little brother, running away from what was thought to be an unseen force, but if you look in the doorway, you can clearly see a figure in what we believe to be a dress.

In the second, is when we were redecorating the house, the picture is taken in the bathroom, at the time the picture was taken to document the wallpaper being removed, but on the stairs you can see a figure watching.

I presume that the little girl is from the orphanage. The poltergeist activity is probably her trying to get attention. Just being playful.

From Jessica Plummer

Dear Richard
A Ghost Story

My brothers, sisters and I used to be told spooky ghost stories just before bedtime by my mother. She used to sit in front of a burning coal fire in an old rocking chair with her favourite patchwork blanket over her legs. We'd all be in our nightwear, sat huddled together upon an uncarpeted floor staring up at her, eagerly waiting to be scared out of our wits.

I remember the atmosphere very well. It was perfect. My mother would always turn off the lights and light a candle to match the mood. She wanted to make sure our hairs stood up on the back of our necks. But most of the time the lights were already off because back then, times were hard.
After lighting a candle on the table next to her, she would then continue to tell us tales of folklore or of any local hauntings in the area. We lived in Dudley, or the Black

Country as it is known to most. And all of my family were born and bred in Dudley, Staffordshire, and you could ask anyone back then if they had a tale to tell about ghosts and they would tell you more than a few. Especially down at the local pub. But mother had not heard many since my father had passed a few years back.

So, as my mother told us the story of the Black Monk of Dudley Castle, the candle would flicker madly, making faceless shadows and inhuman shapes that would dance their way across the walls. Many people would wonder why a mother would tell her children these things. For one, she liked a good ghost story, and two, to stop us creeping out of bed at night. It was a common thing back then. A lot of parents would use this method to stop the kids from getting out of bed. It worked. We wouldn't even get out to go to the toilet. But after knowing what my mother had told me and not experiencing in my lifetime ever seeing a ghost, I then knew she had conned me and my siblings throughout our childhood.

Years later, my mother had passed away and all my brothers and sisters had either married or moved away. I eventually got married and also started a family. I also went straight into work as a builder. The job was good, and it paid well, putting food on the table.

It was 1971 and I remember we had just finished up on a job. We celebrated by going down to the local fish and chip shop and later to the pub. We'd been on this job for a couple of months and now we had to wait for the gaffer to find us a new one. The gaffer soon got back to us regarding a couple who owned an old bungalow. They wanted an extension put on. They'd already got a small one, but they wanted it bigger. So, he told us we had to go and visit the people regarding the work they needed doing.

We spoke to a young couple who were around their mid-thirties. They informed us that they had inherited the building a while back. After discussing the details, we all drove back and went home. The next day, we received the plans from the gaffer regarding what we had to do the property. We headed back out to the bungalow and started work, digging out the footings. We finished all the footings and poured in the concrete. We couldn't do much else until the concrete had dried, so we all popped down to the local pub.

After we had some dinner and a sneaky pint, we went back to the bungalow to check on the concrete. And I remember it as if it were yesterday. As we were checking on the concrete. we all heard the back door to the bungalow open. Standing in the doorway was an old woman.

She was a small lady just under five foot four in height and in her late sixties with hair that was pure white. She was wearing a flowered dress that fell just past her knees. Over the top, she wore a black knitted cardigan that looked as if it had been shrunk in the wash. She started waving her one arm at us and repeatedly telling us to go. We all looked at each other, and we just left as not to cause her any distress. We didn't discuss anything more about it and just reported it back to the gaffer the next day.

Our gaffer went out to see the couple to find out what the problem was and why the work had been halted. When he returned, he told us we all had to go down to the property with him and explain to the couple what had happened and to give them a description of the old woman. We did what the gaffer asked and described everything to the owners about the old lady and what she said. The woman who owned the property went off and fetched a photo. She then asked us all if the lady in the photo who was we had seen. We all nodded. The woman then told us, the lady in the photo was her mother who she's inherited the house from. Her mother who had died nine years before.

We were kind of shocked. And I remember the hairs standing up on the back of my neck as they did when my mother told us those ghost stories. As for the extension, we didn't go back. We were all too scared. I remember us arguing with the gaffer over it. In the end, the extension was finished off by different blokes in the same company. Thinking about it now, it was a terrifying experience. Talking to someone who has been dead for over nine years!

I never believed in ghosts after mother telling us about them when we were kids. I thought it was all codswallop. But now, I guess mother was right.

The number of builders, decorators, plumbers, electricians and demolition men who see ghosts when they are disturbing a building where the previous occupant, although dead is still in residence.

Kenneth J. Baker
(Wolverhampton)

Hello Richard,

My name's Helen, I'll be honest, I have a lot of stories, but I won't bore you with the smaller experiences just a couple of major ones I have had!

The first story I'd like to tell you was back in around 2004/2005 when I lived in a pub, The Two Hands, in Shard End Birmingham. My mom was the licensee and ran the pub with my nan and her partner at the time. I lived above the pub with my mom, her partner, and younger brother and sister. It wasn't in the nicest of areas, but we were used to living in similar areas nearby. The pub stood alone in the middle of a car park, not much to look at but had a bar and lounge, kitchen, cellar and plenty of living space above. As the oldest I chose to have the end bedroom as it was the furthest from my mom's room so I could play music. This seemed like a good idea at the time, yet it was at the end of a very long corridor, I always felt uneasy walking through but nevertheless, I had my own space.

The doors to the upstairs quarters were very heavy-duty doors, but my door wasn't on its hinges which was frustrating, so I had to lean it up against the frame for privacy at night. I used to work a few shifts behind the bar and got to know the local punters, well enough for the stories to begin.

One gentleman did ask if I heard about the security guard who looked after the derelict pub before we moved in. He said, the guard who stayed overnight, once heard an almighty commotion coming from the lounge, so he got out of bed and ran downstairs with his torch and gear thinking people had broken in. When he got to the lounge he was totally confused, as nobody was there. He ran around calling out, checking all doors and windows, but none were damaged or broken, no way of entry whatsoever... yet the tables and chairs were all in a huge pile in the lounge.

I jested with the customer saying it must've been people pranking him or didn't notice they were like it before. He said the guard thought the same and went back up to bed as normal but was woken up again in the middle of the night by an unknown force throwing him from the bed across the room. He apparently fled the scene without returning for his belongings as he was totally terrified. At this point I was intrigued. The customer said, well just be careful, as long as your bedroom isn't the very end one directly above the lounge, you'll be ok.

I'll be honest it freaked me out a little but after a while of being there I forgot about the stories.

I did, however, get extremely frustrated as at least once a fortnight my door would fall down in the middle of the night waking me up in a fright. I would wake up confused and just get out of bed and put it back against the frame and go back to bed thinking nothing of it. I did suffer with anxiety now and then, so my emotions were all over the place, but one night we had a lock in afterhours, so we stayed up and had a few drinks before kicking everyone out and going to bed. I decided to stay behind and clean as it would've meant getting up super early to do it the next day. As I was going to bed, I had that feeling of not being alone. I could just feel it wasn't a person but carried on upstairs to go to bed. I got to the upstairs living quarters in total darkness, I didn't want to wake anybody up so left the lights off and turned to the corridor to walk to my room. That's where I saw him. A figure, darker than the darkness surrounding the area, standing in the doorway of my room at the opposite end of the corridor. Freakishly tall, long coat a possible top hat? I couldn't see any features or colours, just black! I instantly went cold, adrenaline pumping throughout me like electricity, I couldn't move and didn't want to look away. But I knew I had to, I felt if I didn't something bad would happen, what was possibly a couple of seconds felt like forever. I felt the warm splash of a tear on my foot and looked down and straight back up realising I looked away and he vanished!! My room even looked brighter, but I was too terrified to go in so stayed in the living room.

I tried explaining to my mum what happened, and she shrugged it off saying we'd been watching too many Most

Haunted episodes. (Strangely that was our Tuesday night routine, our night together where we would watch Most Haunted and order a Chinese) I did actually feel rather embarrassed so didn't tell many people just the one customer and boyfriend at the time.

From that day I hated going to bed but would make sure I wasn't the last to my room, so all lights were on. It went quiet for a while until the door started falling down again. It became more frequent and annoying as it would also startle my younger siblings from their sleep which caused arguments at home.

My boyfriend's mum had friends round her house one night and we all went over for the night when a gentleman explained he's a medium if anybody wanted readings. I said I would try, although young I was sceptical and didn't know anybody who had passed away for him to pick up on anything, yet he had me hooked.

He held my keys and looked into my eyes and said, "He's angry at you." My heart dropped but didn't have a clue what he meant. He said, "You have the gift, you just don't know how to use it yet, if you need help with it I can mentor you."

I was so confused and still sceptical until he said. "You've experienced moments and spirits or ghosts if you like. It's because you're gifted, and they come to you when your emotions are at the highest or lowest points. It opens up like a gateway for them to contact you. If you want to, you can at any time. But this man blames you for not helping him get to the other side. You saw him; he is not a nice man, in life or death. He's from George Orwell times. He came to you to help him cross over, but you stood scared which he enjoyed. That moment closed that portal down to him and he blames you. Please be careful he's not finished." I mean I'd be lying if I didn't say I was petrified. Nobody knew the ins and outs. He did say more but I'll be honest I was kind of taken aback at that point.

I went home that night and told my mum who was a little more understanding but still on the shelf. That night my door came crashing down as it does, but I checked the time 3:15. The door carried on falling a few times a week from that point at exactly 3:15! I ended up leaving the door away from the frame. We did move out not too long after as I became pregnant with my eldest son.

Another story, again living in a public house, Moby Dick pub Gosta Green Birmingham around Millennium time. Now this place is still standing, and their site even states they have a ghost, so I know the spirits are still very active to this day!

The pub is on several levels. You walk into the first floor, you have stairs down to a cellar, stairs up to an old function room which was never used, then up to the living quarters and there was another building built on the side we called the Wendy House.

The pub was fairly old fashioned, near to Birmingham city center, original uneven wooden floors, the function room had a huge mural painted, you know those kinds where the eyes follow you! There are lots of small stories from a lot of different people about this place.

My dog refused to enter the room I stayed in, I was woken up a few times by my bed being shaken, gusts of wind, people talking when you're alone etc. My dog was a 15-year-old mongrel with epilepsy, just liked to sleep n relax really yet the factory workers next door bought her in the pub after finding her out the front injured. When checking how she got out the front, the only exit was the fire escape top floor which lead onto the roof. Nobody was home to let her out and that's definitely not where we would let her go, it's dangerous even for people.

From then on we would doubly secure the door, yet, not long after, again when nobody was in the private quarters, she fell from the roof, somebody spotted her trying to get back up but unfortunately she had broken her legs.

We were all in a mess and the pub seemed to thrive from it. Now looking back, knowing what I know about how spirits feed from fear, depression, happiness, sadness etc. it makes sense.

We have many photos full of orbs, lights, strange light shapes, movements etc. My mum admits something was definitely around us A LOT! But whoever it was liked my mom and would often help her. She has never forgotten the time she 'thanked a ghost' as we lived at the top of the building. It was 3 stories high, the cellar had a cold room for the barrels and crates of beer, yet the next room was almost a boiler room scorching hot, so we would take our washing into that room to dry.

My mum was carrying a big heavy washing bag over her shoulder down the flights of stairs, she became tired, but the weight completely lifted from her shoulder down the cellar stairs which were totally crooked and dangerous too. She turned to thank her partner at the time, and nobody was there. Not a chance anybody could even run off from that area.

Other times we've heard a music box tinkling around. Fortunately, a couple of times in the function room there have been up to 6-7 people making food in the kitchen area and all heard it and searched everywhere.

My mum allowed a lady, who was in a domestic abuse relationship, to stay with us in the Wendy house until she felt safe. One night my mum's partner and the lady stayed up after hours at the bar to have a final drink when she went quiet and asked my mum's partner if she saw the man? He said, 'no we're locked up and closed'. She explained she watched a man walk down the stairs across the room and straight down the cellar. As you can imagine, he made that poor woman stay up till the sun came up.

More recently, my Nan passed away in August 2017. My mom gave me a ring of my nans, that had a beautiful blue stone, that year for my birthday. I never took it off. Christmas day we had done 'the rounds' visiting people passing gifts etc. and when I got home I realised the stone was missing! I was distraught. We turned the house upside down, retraced our steps, sent out messages but I couldn't face telling my mom. I cried over it every day.

A few months later I was making the dinner and heard a clink on the baking tray, thinking it was ice from the freezer but when I checked it was the stone from the ring!! I have never been so happy. I cried my eyes out. Yet, there was no way possible for it to have turned up at that point, or in that way. I still can't put my finger on how, I just know it was my nan. (I had the ring fixed and put away, too scared to wear again)

If it is true, and I do have 'The Gift', it does explain a lot of strange things that have happened over the years. Even now, the stresses of what's happening in my life are having an effect elsewhere.

I have videos of my dog refusing to enter my boy's bedroom growling and barking at 'nothing'. I have cameras in my boy's room and watch orbs and lights all the time, they complain of seeing a monster in their room, I have watched my youngest talk and touch something that isn't there.

When depressed I would find scratches on my body, 3 scratch marks, just three each time. Shadows, voices, whispers, items disappearing and turning up I could go on! A lot of stuff I do debunk, or make excuses for, anything to stop me being scared at least.

From Helen Lawrence

Hi Richard,

My husband Seamus and I had the absolute pleasure of meeting you and your lovely wife at the "Dining with the Dead". I remembered that you had asked me to send you an email with the story I told you about our encounter many years ago in Derby. Here it is:

Derby Ghost Lights

In April of 2000, my husband and I were in Derby for the ghost walk and dinner at the Derby Gaol. It was a fabulous evening, full of chills, thrills, and fascinating stories about the history and spirit activity in and around Derby. But it was at the end of the evening that proved to be the most chilling of all!
After saying our goodbyes, we exited the Gaol through the back of the building and walked toward where we had

parked our car a couple of streets away. We became aware of an unusual light as we walked along the footpath by the road. It was a wide band of light shining on the pavement, stretching all the way across the road. The light beam was flickering, much like a lamp would look if it were under water. I kept asking, "Where is it coming from?" As the two of us looked up into the trees and nearby buildings for the light's source. I took out my new digital camera. (Remember, this was in 2000!) I put it in video mode to try to capture what we were seeing. My husband can be heard to say, "Can you get it?" And my nervous reply of "Yes, I can get it! I just can't see where it's coming from." Then I panned from the green between us and the back of the Gaol, across the sidewalk and into the street, saying, " It seems to start somewhere over there and goes all the way across the road. I don't know what it is, but it's weird - the ghost lights of Derby!!"

This clip was about 45 seconds long. The quality of it was poor, partly because of the dark, and partly due to the lack of megapixels by today's standards. When we returned home, I must have watched it a hundred times. Upon reviewing the clip on a larger screen, we discovered the flickering seemed more like "percolating" with bubbles that looked like many, many faces!! Also, when I panned over to the green, the video showed a hooded figure clutching the bars of the gate - there was NO ONE seen standing there when we filmed it!!

I'd love to know the history of that little green by the Gaol, as that seemed to be where the light was coming from, and where the figure appeared behind the gate in the video!

From Patti O'Leary

Hello Richard, I saw your request for ghost stories and here's mine.

The Talbot Inn in Belgrave Leicester is opposite Belgrave Hall where Most Haunted visited some time ago. My parents ran the Talbot in the seventies there is a church at the end of the short road between the pub and Belgrave Hall.

The church used to hold faith healing meetings sometimes and when they did a man in a greatcoat and cloth cap would turn up in the off sales room which was to the left of the lounge bar.

My father tells me that when you went to serve him, he would take out his change purse flick through the contents and then walk through the wall to his right into the bar.

When my dad described him to locals, they said that's so and so. Sorry can't remember the name. The off sales used to have a door where the man walked through, and his outfit was described as his demob clothes. My dad wouldn't let any staff try to serve him but one night for a laugh he let the barman go and he nearly screamed the place down. I never saw this, but my dad was used to it and totally unfased.

From Steve Bettany.

Hi Richard,

I am writing in response to your request for ghost stories. Here is mine:

We are from the West Midlands but when I was younger, traditionally as many families from our area did, we always went on holiday to Sand Bay, a short distance from the main town of Weston-super-Mare.

We often travelled to Weston and back down Kewstoke Road, which is quite a densely wooded road.

One night, me (I was probably about seven or eight at the time - I am 43 now), my sister, my Mum and my Auntie were in the car on our way back as normal after a great day in the town.

It was a very stereotypical spooky journey - dark road through a forest, thunder, lightning and rain. I remember distinctly we had to slow shortly before the road bends very sharply onto Beach Road, because there was a fox in the road which was literally like a deer in headlights.

I looked up to the left and said, "what's that?" To which all of us saw a very bright white horse and carriage that seemed out of control, with a man in a top hat and tails cracking the whip furiously as it headed at speed into the bushes before the bend of the road.

Stunned but also with a childish excitement, I yelled 'quick go round the bend and see if it's there' - but as we made our way round, it was nowhere to be seen...
It wasn't the first ghostly experience I'd had, and I've certainly had a few more since!

From Stella Pitt

Hi Richard, it's Martin Gillie.

Here's a ghost story for you. Its written by me but based on a true story from the Baslow area. The cottage where it happened still exists.

DEATH BY BACON FAT...
A Derbyshire tale of woe

In 17th century Derbyshire it wasn't a good thing to be out at night. The moors could be a dangerous and uninviting place. Beeley Moor was no different. A barren, rocky, heather clad place that soaked up the rain and gurgled it out as a boggy mire that would swallow up any lost soul who dared to venture out. A clinging mist would chill the very marrow in your bones.

It was over the moor that a gentleman of the road, a tramp if you will, decided one wintry night to take his chance and fight against the elements. His clothing wasn't designed to withstand the onslaught. His overcoat was held together by string tied at the waist and was battered and torn from years of fighting the elements. His trousers were ripped at the knees and his boots had seen much better days.

Onward the man trudged. He hadn't eaten for 4 days and was driven by the hunger pangs in his stomach. In the distance through the pouring rain he saw a tiny light flickering. Hope of meeting a fellow human being and begging a morsel of food to stave off his hunger drove him forward. His hope of gaining a little shelter in a barn quickened his step. "Soon be there " he thought " soon be there "

The old woman looked out of her cottage window into the darkness. Closing the shutters and drawing up her chair to the fire she gave thanks to the lord for the comfort of her cottage. Slowly she turned the bacon that was sizzling in the pan next to the fire. After a hard day working on her small farm, she was ready for her meal. It was hard running the farm after the death of her husband. And with no family nearby to help she had to do all the work on the farm by herself. Indeed, she had just made sure all the animals were safe in the barns before settling down to cook her own meal.

Who was that knocking on the door? She wasn't expecting visitors and who would venture out on a night like this anyway? " Who is it " she said without leaving her chair. No answer. Thinking it was the wind playing tricks she turned again to face the fire. Again, there was a knock on the door but this time it was a little louder and with it a voice asking for help.

With this the old lady rose from her chair and walked to the old wooden door. Something stopped her from opening the door before she could ask for more information. "Who are you, what do you want? " "A morsel of food please marm if you will, I've been walking these last few days without food or drink and I'm clemmed to the bone "

At this point the old lady remembered what she had heard on her recent shopping trip down to the village. She had been told that another lady had been robbed of all her savings by someone passing through the area, and it wasn't wise to have dealings with any strangers. Remembering this she decided not to open the door and shouted to the visitor to go away. The man pleaded to her but again she refused him.

Enraged by her refusal and with hunger knawing at his gut the man decided to take matters into his own hands. Taking five steps back he ran at the door, screaming his rage and hitting the door full on with his shoulder. The door held fast. Again, he hit it with all the rage and strength he could muster. This time the door gave way and he entered the room.

The old woman put up a valiant fight, but she was no match for this Beast. Even as he prized open her jaw and held her by the throat she continued to fight. It was all to no avail because she suffered a horrible death as he poured the bacon fat down her throat, burning her to death from the inside. The tramp may have got his bacon, but he was caught for the murder of the old lady and for his punishment he was gibbeted alive in a metal cage near the cottage.

His screams could be heard in Chatsworth and as a result the Duke of Devonshire campaigned for gibbeting to be made illegal.

And it is even said today that on certain nights of the year the tramp's screams can still be heard on Beeley Moor

This story has been passed down through generations of Derbyshire folk and the cottage where it happened still exists.

From Martin Gillie.

Dear Richard

In 1992, a friend and I were driving round chatting on our CB radio in Kirk Hallam, when we drove past a car and I said to my mate Dave, 'Hey! check out this old dude in the Cavalier...fast asleep' so we drove up the street and turned round to go back and wake him up, or rather to check on him. We got there (must have been 40 seconds) and there was no one in it, we thought he must have got out and gone inside. It turns out, that the old chap in question, who's car it was, died 2 weeks before......really makes you go cold.
From Mike Bowler from Bideford - North Devon

Hi Richard

Hope this story is what you are looking for. This happened some twenty years ago.

Ours is a strange house. Peculiar things occur; some are shrugged off while others provoke a little more thought. However, one thing stands out which I will tell of now. From where my favourite chair was situated in the far-right corner of the living room as one enters, I had a clear view of the door. Beyond that and on the opposite side of the hall is the stairs which run from my right up to the left as I look at it. The stairs are not the open plan type but are partitioned so that one cannot see the whole of a person as they walk up or down them.

However, if you were to look up to the top right hand side of the door of the living room you would notice that the top of the stair partition is visible giving triangular view created by the slant of that partition and the right angle of door frame thus allowing a small glance as one ascends or descends the stairs as seen from my vantage point.

It was while I was sitting in my chair one evening, around eleven thirty that I became aware of some movement in this area. I immediately looked up but could see nothing. For a few moments I stared into the darkness of the stairwell but convinced myself nothing was there. Now, I have to tell you, I was watching something on the television, something I had been waiting all week to see and can assure you I was wide awake and not in the slightest bit sleepy and, it was again to the television that I returned my attention.

After a short while, and I'm talking no more than a few seconds I became aware once again of movement in the same area. Again, I looked but could see nothing out of the ordinary. This time though I decided to have a closer look and without turning on any of the lights in the hall or stairwell, made my way to the bottom of the stairs and peered up. All seemed as it should be except for the fact that I had that feeling of being watched; a feeling we have all had at one time or another. I returned to my chair.

Two, maybe three minutes passed before something caused me to look once more and it was now that I saw the face staring down at me through the triangular area, I have told you of. Momentarily I froze, my wife was at work and would not be home until the early hours of the morning and I thought it might be our youngest daughter, sleepwalking perhaps. With this thought in mind I averted my eyes so not to wake her suddenly and slowly rose from my chair, the face still visible in my peripheral vision, and made my way through the door, the bottom of the stairs being no more than about four feet away.

Without turning on any lights, as before, I turned and looked up the stairs but, to my surprise the figure had vanished. I made my way swiftly but silently up the stairs. As I passed our son's bedroom, I could see that his door was closed tight and, because it was quite stiff knew I would have heard it open and certainly heard it close again.

I now reached the bedroom of our two daughters and, slowly pushed open the door – they were both fast asleep. Because of the apparent height of the figure in the stairs our eldest daughter would have been too tall to look over the banister standing and too short had she been sitting on the stair. As for our youngest, she could not have got out of bed without making a noise because it was a bunk bed and creaked noisily. But she could not have got back into that bed in such a short space of time.

For a while I waited, if anything were there surely it would manifest itself to me. Nothing! However, I knew I was not alone. This happened three more times in as many weeks and then it stopped.
  Sometimes, just sometimes, I know I am being watched and I am compelled to look for the stranger on the stairs.

From Ron.

New Year's Eve 2012

Myself and my wife don't get out much (With having 3 children) so a family member offered to have the kids for us so we could go to the local pub (The Everest) and see the new year in.

The night was going great, full of laughter and dancing. My wife said she needed the loo, so she popped off and I took the opportunity to have a brief chat with the new landlord (general chit chat).

I was stood at the bar with the ladies toilet to my right and noticed my wife returning, as she walked towards me she looked a little off colour but my instant thought was it's probably all the dancing and food, the very moment she reached me I went to pick my drink up and saw a little girl to the right of my vision (peripheral vision) in an off white dress with very long dark blond hair with her arms around my wife's lower stomach area and head on her.

This startled me as I knew no kids were in the pub that evening so I turned to look at her and she wasn't there!! When I looked straight forward, I could see her again!! Then I leaned forward looked again and nothing then looked forward again but this time nothing.

While I did this my wife was looking at me as though she'd just received the worst news in the world.

I stepped towards her and looked around to the back of her and nothing! No kids anywhere! I stood there shaking my head in disbelief. My wife in a very worried croaky broken voice said, 'what are you looking at?' I said, 'I could have sworn I saw a little girl next to you', she said 'what did she look like?' So, I began to describe her and as I was doing so, she looked like her knees were about to give way! I grabbed her in a supportive manner and asked what was wrong? She said that she had just seen the exact same thing in the mirror in the toilets and I had just described the girl's appearance exactly!

Chills ran down my spine, but it was almost instantly replaced with a feeling of curiosity, I began questioning the landlord and staff about the history, deaths anything! I just wanted answers! But no one was able to help me and this included google too.

A couple of weeks prior to this my wife was complaining of stomach pains and the doctor said it was very possibly an ovarian sist and booked her in for a scan.

The day after the pub her pains were almost completely gone but attended the scan in January anyway. The scan revealed nothing.

So, we were thinking maybe this 'Ghost' was an angel sent to heal her. (We are not even remotely religious)

This experience left me with more and more unanswered questions so as a result I teamed up with a colleague at work in March 2014 and created NP PARANORMAL, myself David (N)ewton and friend Karl (P)orter decided to embark on our own journey to try and get answers to all these paranormal experiences people were having.

So, 4 years later, 200 investigations and 5 domestic cases under our belts we are still searching.

Thanks, Dave NOX PARANORMAL

Dear Richard,

Hello, saw your plea for ghost stories so here are some of mine. I seem to attract ghosts!

When I was about 13, I had two friends round after school. We were on our own in the house, parents still at work and brother still at school. One of my friends said to me "I am sure I just saw someone come up your stairs". So, we had a look- no one there but us. Went back to chatting and a few minutes later the lid of the toilet banged as if someone had lifted it and dropped it. We had another look and there was no-one in the house but us. That would have been about 1973

In 2003 my friend Ann and I were on holiday in St Ives in Cornwall and we did a ghost walk. We walked down a lane the guide said, "walk down there quietly as you might hear a sound you wouldn't expect to". As we walked down, I was sure I could hear horse's hooves but decided it must have been someone's sandals flapping. When we got down to the beach, he told us the legend of a man and a white horse seen on the beach. I whispered to my friend "How funny, I am sure I heard horses' hooves" and he confirmed horses hooves are what had been heard in the lane.

In 2010 my friend Arwen and I stayed at the George and Pilgrims hotel in Glastonbury, in a room called the Monks Cell. When we first walked in, something struck me about the door to the bathroom which was a very gothic looking curved door painted black. At various times we found things had been knocked into the basin from the shelf above, and something I had put in the bin in the bathroom was on the floor. In the middle of the night I woke and could hear noises in the bathroom. I thought Arwen must be in there but when I looked, she was fast asleep in her bed. It was only after our stay that I found out that The Monks Cell is one of the most haunted rooms there.

I also have a ghost cat in my house. I have seen its shadow in the window a few times and seen if out of the corner of my eye. We had a family cat, Trudi, who came to us as a 10-week-old kitten and who lived to be 19 so I am sure it is her.

From Jackie Hewitt of Avalon"

Hiya Richard. My name is Taryn Shrigley.
Here is one of my family ghost stories.

My maternal grandfather was a Grenadier Guard and worked at the Tower of London. He would regularly work the night duty and walked the grounds guarding the Tower. One full moon clear night he was in one of the gardens that contained many statues. As he stood there looking across the quiet moonlit grounds the statues began to move! Their heads turned and looked straight at him as if they were alive! He was so scared that he ran from his post and I am not sure if he was asked to leave or he left voluntarily and became a policeman locally instead.

There were many stories from other guards who walked the parapets of the Tower of London of a headless woman who was often seen by them appearing then disappearing. My great grandma was a medium and psychic and my grandad inherited some of these gifts as have I. Just a short story but genuine all the same. I have attached a photo of my grandad with the plume from his bearskin to this email.

Many blessings Taryn.

Hi Richard,

Our strange encounters began early on in our marriage when we moved into our first house which was in the East Yorkshire village of Patrington. It was the village my family originated from although my husband is from your neck of the woods, Breadsall Village in Derbyshire.

It was a Victorian property but the builder we bought it from had gutted it and taken many of the lovely old features and fireplaces out of it and we think this is where some of the disturbances originated from. Nothing sinister but often in a morning we would come down to find candle sticks balanced upside down on the mantle-piece, ornaments upside down, but carefully placed under the dining table etc. We had bought a lovely old Vienna wall clock from the local antique shop that as soon as the village clock expert had oiled it and hung it on the chimney breast for us, the hands started to go backwards. None of us could believe what we were seeing.

As we started to restore and furnish the house in line with its age i.e. old panelled doors, old fireplaces, dog grates, cornicing etc. All these activities ceased, and we just assumed whoever had lived there in the past approved of what we'd done and that was that or so we thought.

A number of years later by which time I'd had a little boy who was about 4 years old, we were in his bedroom and my son was sticking some stickers in a book when, without looking up, he just said "I hope the old man won't come into my room again mummy...". I tried not to show too much concern because he didn't seem too worried and I didn't want to frighten him.

I asked where the old man had come from and what he looked like and he said he'd come through the wall which his bed was against, that actually backed onto a cottage next door. (The 2 properties differed hugely in age and we found later that there was a window in the bathroom of the next-door house that was about 6 inches from our son's bedroom wall). I asked if he'd gone back through the wall, but he said no, he'd gone onto our landing and disappeared. Apparently, he wore a round black hat, "not a woolly one but a funny one with an edge "which we took to be a bowler hat and he had a walking stick.

We decided not to make an issue of it, nor did we mention it to anyone else least of all to the new residents of the said cottage with whom we became very good friends over the next few years, looking after each other's cats whenever the others were away, excellent dinner parties etc. and no mention of ghosts.

That is, of course, until we moved to another much older house, still within the same village. My son, who was now 8, wanted reassurance that "when you move ghosts don't move with you do they?" so I think there had been more than one visit but he didn't want to talk about it, but obviously understood that what he'd seen was not of this world.

Our friends came to help us move in and we had dinner to celebrate the move and they lost no time in saying "well now you're here we can tell you about the old man that frightened Carol to death in your old house!

Apparently for the last year or so of our time before our move, Carol had been so frightened that when we were away, she would not come into our house in the evening to feed our cats. She somewhat sheepishly admitted that she'd wanted to have a look at what their new pergola looked like from our house because their upstairs windows didn't look out onto that section of their garden, but our son's bedroom window did so she'd nipped upstairs one night when she'd come in to feed our moggies, and gone to have a look through John's window and when she turned to go back downstairs, there was an old man wearing a bowler hat and a suit, complete with walking stick, sitting on our son' s bed. She was understandably terrified and fled so her husband took over from thereon in, not that we went away frequently, but they also decided not to tell us for fear of freaking us out. Also, her husband said that there were issues with the clock when we were not there and neither of them wanted to be there unless they had to. At no point had we ever told them of our son's encounters.

Not long after this, our friends had some family to stay with them at the cottage and Carol's sister woke them all screaming one night because she awoke to find an old man bending over her bed.

They too moved house shortly after this and we do know that the 2 subsequent families living in their cottage, not our old house, experienced frequent activity with this ghost, to the extent that the current occupiers have had some form of exorcism or cleansing. There are various theories, as there always are in village communities, that maybe he was the old doctor, we'll never know, but I've never been brave enough to knock on the door and ask, even though rumour has it that

they did actually discover the old man's identity. Neither have I asked any of the subsequent occupiers of our old house to if there have been any strange goings-on there since we left. All I do know is that no one family has lived there for any length of time. I think I'm happier not knowing!
Best wishes,

From Jane Harper

Hello Richard

I'd like to share a ghost story with you. Several years ago, I went on a 'ghost vigil' at Alton Towers in the hall. We arrived at 8pm for the vigil and were there until 5 in the morning. Nothing much happened while we were there. The people leading it got us to do some different activities to get things moving on. But nothing really happened. That is until we went up the top of one of the towers. There was barely room for all of us and we just about managed to fit in the small space in a circle. We all held hands, all being about 8 of us. We were told to call out to see if anyone was there wanting to make contact, they barely finished saying their sentence when something flicked my head.

I thought I imagined it. We were all still holding hands. no one else said anything. Someone called out again. The flick of the head happened again. This time louder and sharper. My friend standing next to me heard it. But I again shrugged it off. On the final call out, something snapped the strap of my handbag. The handbag was laid across my chest. We were holding hands so no one around us could touch it. But despite this something snapped the strap and made such a loud noise that my friend screamed. I was terrified! I left not long after that. It's hard to describe what it felt like. Much of the evening was, truth be told a bit of a sham/joke and we spent it having a good time but laughing it off. But when I got the flick to the head and the snap of the strap it felt very, very real!

I also had another experience on my own in Jorrocks pub. I was on a ghost walk. I'd not done a ghost walk in Derby before and was enjoying hearing all the tales. Before we got to hear about the Jorrocks ghosts everyone was getting drinks and I went to the ladies toilet. I used the facilities and then tried to unlock the door. But couldn't. I tried again. Again, I couldn't get it to unlock.

I kept trying and trying numerous times to unlock the door. I was starting to panic somewhat. Hoping my friend would realise I was gone and get me out. Then all of a sudden, the lock just opened! It was only after that; did I hear the tale of poltergeist activities in Jorrocks!

Out of interest though the Odeon Cinema at the Meteor Centre. I can't visit there anymore because every time I go, a weird oppressive feeling comes over me and I just can't go back now. My friend wondered if there was any recorded ghost sightings or anything there that could explain my weird experiences in that particular building. I have for sure never had that feeling anywhere else!

kind regards Amy

Hi Richard,

I have a story for you. This one is about an item that was haunted. For our wedding gift many years ago my husband's parents bought us a new cooker. We were thrilled as we were in need of one. I used it for only a short amount of time before it started going wrong. Within a few months we had all the electric elements changed including the hob ones, the clock was also changed.

Every removable part was renewed, some more than once. The engineers were totally stumped with what the problem was. I used to cook cheese pie often, this was the problem dish not that I realised at the time. Something always stopped working when I cooked this for tea hence all the new bits! One afternoon I decided to cook cheese pie for tea, I cooked the potatoes, grated the cheese mixed it all up, put it in an oven dish put in the oven then bang. The RCD cut out. I turned the RCD switch back on turned the oven on and bang off it went again. I reset it again and tried it again for it to go bang but this time as I turned the cooker back on I held the switch, there was such a huge bang it threw me across the kitchen. My daughter came running in, she rang my husband at work who rushed back home. The next thing I know I was waking up in hospital. No idea how I got there at the time. The doctors said I had had a big shock off the cooker. I never cooked cheese pie again after that and it never cut out again.

From Gill Pakes

Dear Richard,

Here is my story of my first house in Manchester Street, Derby. I miss it but in hindsight I don't miss the feelings of never quite being alone!

From this experience I really believe that our ties to our family never really leave us even after we have left this earth.

One gloomy day in November in 2006 I was about to go on my lunch break and thought I'd walk around the area and have a look at the surrounding streets to see what houses were for sale.
I was looking to buy my first house, newly single and turning 30
I was looking for somewhere central in town that I could call my own not far from the office I was working at as at the time I didn't drive so needed to be central.

It started to drizzle so I thought I'd just walk down a couple of side streets and then head back. I turned off the main road and walked down a terraced street with most properties rented to students, I thought this isn't really the area that I would want to look at purchasing a house but I felt a vague familiarity as I passed the derelict mill at the end of the road and I was intrigued as I had never been here before, yet I had a strange feeling that there was a cobbled area with outbuildings further up the street between the terraced houses.

Curiosity got the better of me and I decided to carry on up the street just to see if I was right and then I would head back to the office and Google the area and see what's for sale in the locality.

As I walked the drizzle became rain just as I came upon 3 outbuildings set back from the road in a cobbled area! How odd I thought, that's what I thought would be there!

Suddenly I became aware of a man in overalls, cap and a dark coloured jacket with patches on the elbows leaning in the corner between a wooden door to a car restoration workshop and the wall of a terraced house, he was covered in grease and smoking a very strong cigarette (interestingly thinking back it was the cigarette I smelt first, before I saw him).

He made me feel a little uneasy as he looked at me and said "ow do"

Nervously I said that I wasn't expecting the rain and that I was just exploring the area as I was looking to buy a house but that I better get back to work, I turned to walk back when he lurched forward making me feel a bit jumpy, then slowly tapped the wall of the terraced house with his hand holding the cigarette and said tipping his head to one side you should buy this, it's for sale.

I thanked him and made my excuses and walked rather quickly up the street, not wanting to look back but feeling like he was watching me leave.

Back in the warm and dry I ate my lunch and tried to shrug off the strange uneasy feeling and scolding myself at how daft I was wandering around an area I didn't know on my own.

Later on the bus home, I couldn't stop thinking about the street and why it felt familiar, I googled the area and found that the mill and the surrounding streets belonged to a brewery in the late 1890s, the house by the outbuildings was indeed for sale and had been for a long time (although there was no sign up) and it was well below my price range and needed a lot of work but strangely it had a pull about it that made me more interested.

I went to bed that evening and it was all I could think about, my dreams flitted from the familiarity of the mill and the street I had never been to before, then back to the house, but always the man in the jacket was just there in the background. Having not slept very well during that night, the next morning I took the bus to work and stopped in the estate agents I'd googled, to ask about the property. They were surprised and said they could show me round that lunch time.

I met the estate agent. A smart chap with a clip board, younger than me who introduced himself and opened the door to the property, he said cheerily "I'll wait here, you have a good look round" I thought this was strange and walked into the front room. It was like going back in time, gorgeous fireplaces, original wooden floor to ceiling cupboards, pine doors, as I walked into the huge middle room and opened the shutters on the window I smelt a peculiar damp smell peppered with thick cigarette smoke, despite this I was in love with the house!

The stairs had a strange feeling about them, but I soon forgot about this when I saw the original Victorian fuse box at the top of the stairs the house was perfect.

I stood looking out of the window at the estate agent on the pavement below wondering what would be a sensible offer and should I wait until I'm back at work to put the offer in? I saw a few students walking up the street with pizza from the pizza place on the main road, handy I thought and there was the man in the jacket, perhaps on his lunch break, cigarette in his mouth, standing across the road from the estate agent, arms behind his back leaning against the front of the house across the road. Neither had seemed to acknowledge each other but he looked up at my window, I waved, I'm not sure he saw me. I thought that I must thank him for telling me about this house. It's like I was meant to live here! I loved it!

My offer was accepted, my family thought I was mad, and there was so much work to do on the property (new heating system, new electrics, damp proofing, lead water pipes removed!) But undeterred I moved in during the February and work commenced on modernising the place without removing the original features.

The house did feel odd at times, I had an electrician and a plasterer leave halfway through their jobs and never return for their payment and they wouldn't even return my calls!

A plumber mentioned that the house had a strange feeling and he didn't like being on his own there (just as well as he did some work while I wasn't in and I thought he must have chain smoked the entire time he was there! The house smelt so strongly of cigarettes) but I always felt like I was meant to be there, my cat would jump odd times and stare at the stairs, I took on lodgers to help pay the mortgage and they never stayed too long citing that they felt uncomfortable living there but I belonged there, I was home.

After about a year I started dating someone who would eventually become my husband. One evening he was staying over and said he would start cooking tea (an M&S dine in for £10!) while I had a shower. He was in the kitchen (I had converted the outside toilet and coal shed for more space). He suddenly felt uneasy as he turned he saw what he reported to the police as, a man with dark hair in a jacket with patches on the elbows enter the middle room through the original outside door, my boyfriend shouted and as he followed, the man walked up the stairs, turned and smiled at my boyfriend, he had grease on his face and a cigarette in his mouth.

My boyfriend ran at the stairs fearing something would happen to me in the shower. I heard my boyfriend scramble on to the landing. The smell of cigarette smoked filled the air and set the newly installed smoke alarm off!

"What the bloody hell has happened" I said dripping wet on the landing. My boyfriend was already telling the police operator that we had been broken into, that the man was still in the house. I grabbed my clothes.

The Police arrived and searched everywhere including the attic and cellar to see if he could have left the house any other way, the police said he must be hiding somewhere, and they searched the house thoroughly. No one was found. We were advised to stay somewhere else that evening, we went to my boyfriend's house and my boyfriend refused to stay at my house again.

In time I fell pregnant and we moved into my boyfriend's house permanently. I tried to rent my property, but no one would stay more than a few months.

I loved that house it was strangely part of me but with a small child, one on the way, a wedding to plan and another mortgage I knew I couldn't keep it. We prepared the house for sale but hadn't instructed an estate agent yet, the time just didn't feel right I had now owned the house for 12 years, it had been empty for 3 years but I just couldn't bring myself to list it with an agent.

One summer day I went to cut the grass, my husband came to pick me up but before leaving I sat on the stairs, I cried and said out loud how sad I was to leave but how happy I was to have been part of the house and its history. I thought to myself how thin the walls must be and how much the students next door must smoke as it comes though the bricks!

The smell was very strong in the middle room that day, but I was pregnant with my second child and I seemed very sensitive to smells having a bad case of morning sickness!

I got everything together, wiped my eyes and locked the front door. As I stepped back onto the pavement I walked into a man in his 30s, I apologised for treading on him, he smiled and said he was looking to buy a house in the area and he had been taking to a man at the outbuildings next door, he said, you will be selling the house soon.

I smiled, unlocked the door and said "have a look round if you want, I'll wait here" he did.

My husband and little boy watching from the car thought I was bonkers but I gave him my number and he walked off up the street, I got in my husband's car and as I pulled off, I saw the man in the jacket smoking a cigarette by the side of the house. He is always watching I thought, I waved, he smiled.

Later that day I sold my house to the man I stood on, it felt right, he made an offer and I accepted. Everything went through the solicitors and when the day came to hand over the keys I had just commenced maternity leave with my second baby so we decided to take my 98 year old grandfather out for lunch as myself and my husband were both off work.

We arranged to meet the new owner at the house at midday on route to the restaurant having picked up my grandfather. He had never seen my first house so I thought it would be nice to show him where I had lived. The new owner was waiting excitedly outside the house, we pulled up and parked at the outbuildings, I left my grandfather in the car with my children and husband and handed over the keys by the front door. I wished him well and he said that he thought the house had chosen him as he wasn't really looking in this area, but the house was wonderful. I joked "that's how I felt, we must be related". We laughed.

I got back in the car and I took one last look at my first home tinged with happy sadness, when I first saw the house I was single and carefree now I was married, a mother of two boys caring for my elderly grandfather, how things change and move on but I was so happy that the person who bought it was so much like me.

My grandfather spoke and visibly jolted me from my thoughts. "It's been years since I was on this street, your great great uncle was given a house with his job at the mill here." "Aye, I remember going on my dad's crossbar cycling from Chaddesden to see him, he'd be leaning smoking a fag, watching the world go by" "filthy he would be grease all over his face, in his patched jacket and cap, never took them off always having a smoke"

My husband went pale, I looked round at the house, the outbuildings and mill (now converted into luxury apartments) as they slowly disappeared out of view.

"He'd have liked you all" my grandad said.

I replied, "How strange grandad, that I would end up on the same street!" "I wish I had met him I think I would have liked him too"

We carried on to the restaurant and have never spoken about it since.

I still miss my first house, we have moved to a 1930s house now but sometimes, in a fleeting moment we think we can smell a familiar smell and we smile at each other.

From Amy Garratt

Hi Richard,
I just wanted to tell you of my first ghost and what got me interested in the paranormal

I saw my first apparition when I was just 10 years old, I was asleep in my bed and my sister was sleeping in the same room as me, and also saw the apparition. In fact, she saw it first.

She woke me up and told me to look towards the bedroom window. As I looked, we both saw the spirit of an old lady, looking out of the window, she was wearing a mop cap, a long skirt and blouse. We both sat and watched her for what seemed like ages, we were whispering to each other hoping not to disturb her. Well, while we were whispering about the lady, she turned to face us, and she gave us a big smile and just vanished before our eyes. Neither of us told anyone, until many years later when we spoke of it again to each other, and that is when our father told us of a lady who had passed away in our bedroom waiting for her husband to return from somewhere and he never did return home.

Since this I have had pets that have died and followed me wherever I went. I have seen shadow figures and my love of all things paranormal have gone from strength to strength. Unfortunately, I don't have a photo of this incident as we did not have mobile phones or a camera, also my father would not let us use his camera.

From Arianne

Hello Richard,

My ghost stories from when I worked in Somerset House, London, which is reputedly haunted by Lord Nelson.

During my time working there I saw two full bodied apparitions. I often worked in a basement storeroom where I always felt that I was being watched. On one occasion I had my back to the door but as I turned around, I saw the apparition of a man in his 40s, wearing brown trousers and a reddish-brown jumper watching me. I was debating whether to speak to him but after a couple of minutes the apparition vanished. I went outside to check the corridors just in case it was another member of staff, but no-one was there.

On another occasion I was in a kitchen where I caught a glimpse of a man in a long white dress drifting past me and heading towards the ladies toilets which were situated close by. Again, I went to check the toilets, but no-one was in there.

There is an area in Somerset House called the Dead House, which contains tombstones embedded in the walls. I was walking through there one summer's day to get to another part of the building. I managed to miss the turning and ended up at the back of the passageway. I turned around to walk back and then heard the door at the end of the corridor closing. I turned back around to look and could see the door closing by itself. The door was solid, over an inch thick and there was no breeze or other way which could have caused it to move by itself.

Other former colleagues have witnessed unusual occurrences there as well. A colleague was working around 6pm one night and went to use the toilet (this was close to where I saw the apparition of the man). She heard the taps go on by themselves even though no-one else was in there. Another colleague went into a basement room where he saw the figure of a man sat at an antique desk. Someone else saw a man sat in a chair in one of the conference rooms and also chairs moving around in there (they didn't describe the

figures so I can't say if it is the same figure as the man who I saw).
Security caught a figure of a woman in white on CCTV (unfortunately I never saw this). It happened in a different wing to where I saw the woman in white, however there is a possibility it could be the same figure.

From Cheryl Martin

Dear Richard, I live in the country near Bath.
I was driving to the next village one evening about 7pm. As I drove along a straight stretch of road, I noticed a male figure standing on the grass verge almost in the road, as I passed him, I thought he was waiting to cross. Looking in the rear-view mirror I realised he was dressed strangely in some sort of uniform, helmet and holding a Pike.

I though perhaps it was someone in fancy dress but as I looked back, he was gone, no sign at all.

I mentioned it to my husband when I got back, he said it sounded like a Roundhead soldier, I looked it up on the internet and he was correct.

I thought it was strange that he had disappeared so quickly and started to wonder if it was a ghost I had seen. Further research showed that there is a

property nearby that was used to house injured soldiers from the Battle of Lansdown Hill Bath, which is approximately 7 miles away from us.
I'm now convinced it was a ghost as the figure was not clear but hazy, if he had crossed the road I would have still been able to see him walking along the verge as there was a solid hedge which would stop anyone disappearing.
Ghost or my imagination!

From Kate Cook
Hi there Richard, here is my story...

I'm a huge believer in the stone tape theory and so is my family. It took place in my house in Chesterfield, where my grandmother saw something strange. She was babysitting myself and my little brother one evening with my grandad and decided to make a cup of tea, like elders often do and she happened to glance into the living room from the kitchen only to see a bald man in a white shirt and black trousers bending down at the fireplace and he simply vanished in the blink of an eye
...she said she was frozen cold as it made her jump a little. We later did some research to find on my street before the houses were built circa 1987 there once was allotments, we believe the old man used to live there and grow his plants. The story doesn't end there...my mum was on a webcam chat with friends in New York and they asked her " is your dad with you?" And my mum replied "no, everyone is in bed I'm the only one up" and they described what they saw...a bald man in a white shirt and black trousers just drift behind her, the same man my grandmother saw. She said she felt an ice-cold draft behind her around the time they saw the figure. Poltergeist like activity often happens in my house with cups

rattling and hairbrushes flying onto the floor...it all seems to happen around Christmas time.

From Ben Stocks

Hi Richard, I live in a ground floor flat on a previous site of Gate Studios in Borehamwood Herts. Gate Studios was investigated by the one and only Derek Acorah on Most Haunted.

We have lived here for 11 years now with many things happening from clothes being tugged, being scratched, a young child walking through the kitchen table straight through the wall and a dark figure rushing out the bathroom. I often wonder if our neighbours have seen or experience anything.

From Anita Murphy

Hi Richard,
Here is one of my brushes with the paranormal.
(If you could mention my name Daniel Williams, 47 - King Charles I return)

In 2017 I heard about the Kings Arms Hotel in Stow-on-the-Wold, Gloucestershire.

It is known that King Charles I stayed there before the battle of Naseby in 1645.
In the market square opposite the hotel is a memorial to the battle that happened there between Royalists and Parliamentarians in 1646.

It was a bloody battle under 1000 were said to be killed and around 1000 Royalist Prisoners were taken in the outcome when they surrendered.

I had done some brief research before arriving. Reading that a particular street had been named after a combination of the words 'duck' and 'bath'. A reference to an area of the battle where the fighting was so violent that ducks bathed in pools of blood on the street.

That night my friend and I whilst walking up a street could smell a strong burning smell with a hint of decay. Seemed unusual given there weren't any obvious fires burning around.

The smell lingered heavily in the air and smelt quite old in my own way of interpreting it.

A lady just happened to be walking down the road about to go into her property. I stopped her and asked if she could smell the burning odour too and her reaction was a resolute no and a look back of bemusement.

That night I went to bed in the room King Charles is said to have slept in. During the night I had a horrible vivid and somewhat disconcerting nightmare of a vicious dog snarling at me. It's jaws dripping. To my mind it felt like a dream that someone from the 17th Century may have had with the imagination and folklore back then.

After eventual sleep, the next day came. I said to my friend I need to try and find this street that was quoted as saying many were slaughtered there, so I could stand there, say a prayer, and pay my respects.

A google search brought up a shock. The street I had smelt the decaying smell of burning was in fact Digbeth Street- named after the horror that happened there!

It was then that I realised the smell was in fact something paranormal and must be linked to death. Other people in the past have reported similar smells at other sites throughout history/investigations.

I said my prayer and duly left Stow-on-the-Wold. It was a touching visit. Such was the impression it left on me.

A day or so passed and one evening was about to enter my bedroom where in the hallway I stopped with surprise as I smelt the pungent smell I had discovered back in Stow! Calling my housemate, he too could smell it.

My visit to Stow on the Wold did not go unnoticed it seems, but I know who ever watched and followed me back to my home knew I had the memory of their trauma and sacrifice in my heart.

From Daniel

Hi Richard, I have a story for you if it interests you.

Many years ago, I met a man whilst at work, he was a customer in the garage I worked at. Over time we got to know each other, and he asked me out for afternoon tea. We chatted for some time, he told me in depth what he did for employment. I was a little taken back when he told me he was a Doctor in healing. I'm surprised I didn't pick this up as I'm a medium. He told me I was suffering health wise with a condition I've had no help for. He was right, I suffer from Fibromyalgia. He explained about the healing center he works at and invited me to have some healing. I did go a few times for healing and picked up on quite a few spiritual energies. This one time we were leaving but stopped to talk to the owner's wife who was in the office.

Stood behind her was a slim lady in what I can only describe wearing 50s style clothes. I tried to involve her in the conversation with funny looks from my friend David and the owner's wife. I thought it strange as they are not rude people. We waved bye but again David ignored the lady. She was waving us goodbye, I said goodbye to her but still David said nothing. We got into the car before I asked him who the lady was, he told me there was no one in the office with the owners wife.......

From Gill Pakes

Hi Richard,

When my dad had a major heart attack in 2005 (it was unlikely he would survive), he was in A&E before treatment and a Middle Eastern gentleman came up to his bed and told my dad that he would be ok and not to worry. Dad recounted this to several staff and consultants on duty who confirmed there was no one on duty with that description and no known doctor of that description. He has been fine ever since.

On another occasion, my father was working on an empty property in the South Hams (Devon) as a painter and decorator and the phone kept ringing every time, he was in the property but on answering the phone no one was there. On the last day he complained to the Owner that the phone kept ringing and was told there was no live telephone connection to the property.

From Sam

Dear Richard

The Richmond Arms Hotel, Tomintoul. Built in 1856 as a Fishing lodge for middle class gentlemen, but not their wives. In its early days, the only females permitted were the housekeeping and kitchen staff.

Our family, staff and guests have all had experiences within the building, and not just isolated to one particular area, but to many areas, except the newest part of the building that was added in the 1980's. Because of this we started a ghost book for guests to write any experiences in for other to see, comment on and in some cases for amusement.

When guests have left for the day, and the hotel is almost empty, voices have been heard coming from rooms. Now at first we thought that was down to a TV or radio being left on, but on entering the room, TV was off and the voices stopped, one of the most common rooms for this to happen is room 19.

A lady who was staying in room 14, reading her book in bed, while her husband took a bath, felt a stroking sensation on her leg. This was the guest who suggested the ghost book.

When we took over the hotel, it had been shut for 3 years, and we spent 6 months getting it reopened. The hotel had suffered damage from a previous tenant and the long cold winters in Scotland. When we did re-open, we had a lot of rooms we were unable to use because of the damage. One section we used, rooms 10, 11 and 12. My husband and I were in room 10. One night I was in bed and the door opened and I thought it was my husband coming to bed, I felt someone watching me, I couldn't move. I once did an investigation with a group called Haunted World and they posted a video on YouTube from room 14. The camera was left running and it was being moved. You can also hear a cat, which we did not have at that point.

While my husband was repairing the hotel, he was up a ladder outside room 10, and he saw what he believed to be a chambermaid coming from room 12 to room 11. In a morning he often sees a stable boy riding a horse down the Public Bar. This bar was added to the hotel and was originally the side street to the stables at the rear of the hotel. A staff member's son, said that he had been talking to a boy in the laundry called Alfie, which is in the old stables. My husband's shoelaces were always being untied when he walked down the rear passage to the laundry. He also sees a man waiting to be served in the public bar at a nighttime.

From Sonia Hutchinson Pendlebury

Dear Richard,

My story is based at Tutbury castle.

I did a sleep over for charity in 2007. We did a walk around of the castle and grounds. It was during a talk with Lesley in her full Mary Queen of Scott's costume. She randomly called people forward. I watch as people step up and hold their hand in mid-air feeling for cold spots. When she made eye contact with me. She called me forward and told me to hold my hand out and slowly feel around the air.

It was at that moment all the hairs on my arm stood up and I was overcome with sadness. I looked up at Lesley and she said, 'My Darling, you can feel her can't you'.

Through the sadness and tears I said, 'Yes I can feel her'. As I stepped away, all the sadness left, and I felt as if I'd had a strange experience.

Later that night we did a silent séance in the kings bedroom when all of a sudden, I saw a beautiful shiny shimmer walk right in front of me. As if it was a beautiful long gown. I let out a gasp. No one else had seen it but the gentleman who was our guide for the evening knew exactly what I'd seen.

From Lisa Marie Davies.

Hi Richard,

There are 2 things I want to tell you.

The first is my dog Jack and my dad. My dad was almost bedridden for a year before he died in 1999. He would get out of bed at 7.30pm every night, come to the living room and ask, "are we having a brew?"

When dad died, I bought myself a puppy, a wire fox terrier called Jack. A few nights into my 13 years with Jack he started to look towards the living room door at 7.30. Then he would get up and eventually over the course of a few weeks he would bark at the door. Not only barking but backing away into the room as if someone was coming into the room. This went on for months, 7.30 every night.

One night both mum and I were watching tv and we both heard my dad shout "are you there?" At exactly the same moment. She shouted "yes", and I was up out of my chair when we realised. We looked at each other in shock and surprise.

The other thing is the story of John Henry the farm hand at the Blue Lion at Cwm in North Wales.

Mum used to work there, and she would come home and talk about John Henry. She described him as a young man wearing a sack round his shoulders and his trousers tied round his knees with string. He was always walking through the car park towards the church on the other side of the road. He knew she was there, but it didn't seem to bother him, nor did he interact with her but he was aware. Now if you spoke to anyone round there at the time you would get various stories, he was a child, an old man, wearing monks robes or a waistcoat, but mum was adamant about his string tied knees.

From Sam

Dear Richard,

My name is Ryan Spencer, I am 35 and, like yourself, am a resident of Derby.
I would like to share with you an experience that happened to me when I was around 12 years old.

In the years since this occurred, I have, of course, matured somewhat and as you would expect the perspective of certain events from our childhood change as we grow, and we view those events in a different, more lateral context. This is certainly true for me and my experience as I have always kept an open mind, but I still find what happened to me none the less intriguing.

I grew up in the village of Ambergate, a mere 11 miles north from the city of Derby. The house I lived in with my parents and younger sister was a three bed terrace situated at the top of Newbridge Road, a steep incline that I had to descend and ascend every day to make the journey to and from the school bus.

At the back of our house, and others that lined our road, lay the fields where myself, my sister and our shared friends would play most days during the summer, climbing the trees by the dry stone wall at the edge of the field with this stunning scenery all around. I consider myself the luckiest person on earth to have had that space as our playground.

It was these fields that were to play a significant role in an experience that happened to me in 1996.

I can't be sure of the exact dates that the following experiences occurred on, but I can tell you that it took place sometime during the height of summer.

My mum had gone to Paris for five days with her friend to take in the art at the Louvre, so my sister and I had been left at home with our dad.

The night in question must have been a fairly warm one as I remember that I was struggling to get to sleep so I just lay on my bed looking up at the ceiling.

My room was at the back of the house and if you looked through the window during the day you would be able to see the fields I mentioned earlier.

My sisters room was also at the back of the house at the end of the corridor and actually closer to the fields compared to my room.

I'm very sure that both my dad and sister were fast asleep at the time as it was fairly late, most certainly past 11pm and the house and its surroundings were very quiet, which was pretty normal considering our location.

As I lay there listening to the eerie silence I was suddenly alerted to what can only be described as a blood curdling scream which went through me like a frosty wind and for a moment it was if my heart had stopped.

As you would expect any 12-year-old to process what was happening my initial thoughts turned to the supernatural.

The scream itself was identifiable and due to the tone and pitch I would have said it had belonged a female child of around 8 to 10 years old but what shook me even more is that it appeared to have come from the field directly at the back of the house facing my bedroom window.

Seconds passed as I tried to rationalise what I had heard in order to feel more comfortable and against my better nature I plucked up the courage to go to the window and peer outside.

Timidly pulling the blind aside I looked out into the night; below my window I could just make out the back yards of our house and our neighbours, but no lights were on, so it was hard to see anything. I looked a little further into the gardens but again there was hardly any light, so nothing stood out and beyond the gardens, behind the sheds the field was indiscernible, a complete abyss.

I put my blind back down and went back to my bed with a sigh and decided that there was a reasonable solution to what I had heard.

About five more minutes passed and I began to feel more at ease and was making an attempt to try to go to sleep when to my horror the scream came again and this time all rationality deserted me and I ran out of my room and, to my shame, began crying in the corridor outside.

It was at this point that my dad and my sister heard me and came out to see what was wrong. I tried explaining what had happened to my dad but was met with some frustration and sent back to my room. Luckily though I did not hear the screams again.

It has been noted by those I have recounted my story to that the screams I heard could have in-fact come from a fox as they have been known to make similar noises, a theory that, as an adult, I could accept if it wasn't for the event that took place the following year.

The rest of the year came and went and before you knew it was summer again, but the memory of my experience was still ripe in my mind and it wasn't long before an idea came to me.

A couple of years earlier my Grandad had taken me into town to spend my birthday money and I came back with a dictation machine, a small hand held tape recorder that a novelist might use when a moment of inspiration hits them while out and about. With that in mind I, along with my sister, went into the field one afternoon before sunset to see if we could maybe capture an EVP.

There was a fair breeze blowing through the grass and the trees as we circled the field, machine in hand and on record. Every now and then, when we hit a certain area of the field, I would ask a couple of statutory questions that any good ghost hunter would ask including "is any one there?".

After about 40 or 50 minutes of roaming around we decided to call it a day and headed back to the house and we went straight to my room to review what we had just recorded.

Having rewound the tape, I pressed play and turned up the volume on the recorder and held it close to our ears. For about half an hour we listened intently, the sound of the wind distorted the recording, but you could still clearly make out the crunching of our feet through the grass and, of course, the questions I had asked.

We were about three quarters of the way through the recording and were beginning to think we had been unsuccessful in our attempt to record an EVP, not that we were too disappointed as we hadn't really expected to capture any kind of anomaly. But to our shock, we did.

Though the wind played an integral role in the recording you couldn't mistake the discernible plea that whispered to us in a voice that sounded like that of a female child of no more than 8 to 10 years of age, it said "help me, please help me".

It's fair to say that the hairs on the backs of our necks stood up as we tried to comprehend what we had just heard through the tape recorder.

I remember we played it back to our mum and you could tell when she heard it that, she too, was shocked though she tried to hide it.

Unfortunately, the tape recorder has been lost to time, I think it probably got chucked out when my parents moved out and went their separate ways but even as rational adults my sister and I have reminisced about that day and still find the experience a bit chilling.

From Ryan Spencer

Dear Richard,

Staff at a Belper nursing home have reported unusual goings on after the passing of a resident whose room was on the upper floor of the building. Footsteps have been heard coming from the empty rooms above them as they worked on the floor below, when they went to investigate they have felt a coldness even though the heating was on and the chandelier swinging even though there was no breeze or open windows.

A couple staying in a room on the third floor of an old country house B&B near Eyam reported seeing flashes of light in their room during the night, flashes too bright and short to have come from a mobile phone. They were frequent but random and could not have come from outside due to the thickness of the curtains and appeared to have no fixed origin within the room itself.

A lady in her home after a short illness rose from her bed and crossing the landing of her home to answer a ringing telephone, saw a figure at the bottom of the stairs that looked very much like the mother of her friend. As she answered the phone it was her friend to tell her that her mother had died the previous evening in her sleep. The same lady woke during the night on a separate occasion to find a figure standing at the bottom of her bed, this being the figure of her husband's father, an hour later her mother in law telephoned to say that her husband had locked himself in the bathroom and passed away.

Anonymous

Hi Richard

Just after my grandad died in 1984, I went from home in Bedford to visit my grandma in Burnley, Lancashire by bus. On route in Manchester I had my purse stolen. I still got to Burnley and grandma was naturally concerned but it seems also was my late grandad whose bedroom I slept in that night. It was an old weavers cottage like the ones on Coronation Street and the bathroom was a later addition to the bedroom. I woke in the night and saw the outline of my grandad walking across the room to the bathroom as had been his habit for many years. It was definitely his shape but two dimensional. I pinched myself and closed my eyes and opened them again, but he was still there making his slow progress across the room. He was of military bearing, somewhat stout, a distinctive man I couldn't have mistaken him.

Secondly when my two sons now adults were much younger, we were on holiday visiting Battle Abbey.

I was alone with the children in the play area which was among old trees and had a bit of an atmosphere. I gradually became aware of an unmelodic chanting of untrained male voices and it struck me that it was odd if it were a record or a performance, they would be better singers. When I tried to analyse it the music faded, and I asked my older son if he had heard anything he hadn't. But then it came back again and eventually stopped. I think it was coming from the direction of an old monastery and the untrained voices were those of new novice monks from the village centuries earlier.

Best wishes Stella Williamson

Hi Richard,

Here's two stories from me for your collection.

Although true events as much as I recall (and you do tend to remember such detail in a paranormal encounter, oddly).

The Dapper Gentleman

From 1980-1992, my formative years were spent in the urban suburb of Tilehurst in Reading.

As I was growing up and hit about 6 or 7, I became aware that local legend had it that there was the spirit of a Victorian man that was in the woods and would occasionally jump out at children. Naturally, my friends and I dismissed it out of hand.
Some 12-18 months later though, we found 'him'. As with many true paranormal incidents, it happened in bright

sunshine on a hot August day, rather than in the dead of night.

About 4 or 5 of us were playing near our den that we had constructed over the early part of the summer holidays. We then became aware of a rustling in the undergrowth behind us. From nowhere, a man emerged and came towards us. I think we would have been afraid of normal adult authority anyhow, but despite our young age, we all knew that this chap didn't 'fit' with his surroundings.

He was about seven feet tall (although to a small child, anyone over 6 feet was rather tall) and a white, adult male. He looked like he was out of a circus. A top hat adorned his head, but he was dressed in a red and black stripped cloak with black trousers. He had a trimmed beard and carried a wooden cane. He never spoke at any point.

Suffice to say we all ran for our lives. Even at such a formative age, we had a basic understanding that people just didn't 'appear' out of nowhere.

I told my parents of the encounter, but they just laughed and dismissed it as a child's imagination. However, we knew what we saw!

And see him again, we did. Well, two of us. It was roughly the same time of year again a few summers on. This time, my parents were away on holiday and my grandparents were looking after us. My friend and I had been playing in the woods on our bikes, quite close to the spot where our den had been previously. Then it suddenly became quite cold, and the smart chap came again. As we had bikes, we were rather confident that we could outpace him if required. He walked towards us and we scampered a little way away, keeping him in view. Still he headed toward us. We eventually got towards the edge of the wood and near to the path that led home and in a built-up area. The man who was following then seemed to 'jump' up into the trees. We could not believe our eyes. He then came down and was much closer to us. It was almost like a demonstration of 'look what I can do if I really want to'. We cycled hard and he followed. Upon reaching the main concrete path, he came out of the woods in his full regalia and 'faded out' so that no-one and nothing was there.

Somewhat perturbed by the events, my friend and I made our separate ways home. I told my grandparents about what we had witnessed and they took it all in; rather than laughing they offered that perhaps Springheeled Jack was also in Reading, or some version of him (being from that area of London, they had heard of the manifestation). I have since researched into him, and although there are some similarities such as the mannerism and ability to leap over buildings (or trees in our case), the dress was very different. It is totally inexplicable and even now I wonder if perhaps it was a hallucination between several people! Perhaps though, it was a form of time travel that we are just unaware of in the present day?

The Glowing Dog

Around 2002, I was driving to my parents' house in Gloucestershire from Somerset where I now lived.

I had been working a very late shift in a supermarket and it was about 2am as I made my way across the A39 towards Bridgewater, where I could get the M5 straight up to Glos.

At Cannington, which is a well-known stretch of road that plays host to a phantom hitchhiker, I reached a junction when I heard a screeching noise of car tyres.

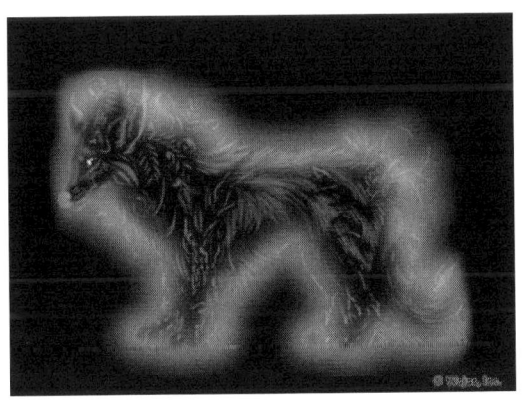

As I was literally in front of the junction, which had a hedge to the left of my car, a glowing white dog appeared to jump from the inside of the hedge and right into the path of my car. I slammed the brakes on and hit it but did stop. There was no impact, however. At the immediate same time, a car came careering out of the junction right into my path, with a load of drunken teenagers in it. Had I not have stopped for the dog, the car would have come straight into my driver's door, and there would have been a very serious accident.

The car clipped the hedge and carried on its merry way towards Bridgewater. I got out of my car to inspect the damage and see if the dog was okay (fearing the worst), but there was nothing there. No dog, no impact, no damage. I looked under the car and all was fine.

It's completely inexplicable but I do know that without the phantom saviour, the outcome could have been much worse that night.

From Graham Philpot

Dear Richard,

In 2006 my sister and I took a short break in Oban, Scotland One day we visited Dunstaffnage Castle, beautiful place so we were taking lots of pictures.

Being in a playful mood we decided to try and create 'Where's Clare' pictures (like 'where's wally') which involved me (Clare) hiding in plain sight amongst the castle ruins, peeping out from behind things. Obviously, I wasn't camouflaged very well, and it was just a bit of fun. We had a great day and stopped at a small pub on our way back to the hotel for a drink. Out came the camera and as we were pouring over the photos from our day, giggling at the deplorable efforts at hiding, one picture in particular caught our attention. It was a picture of me peeping out from behind a huge old door and at first glance it looks like part of my leg and arm are also showing. But what caught our attention was that the clothing showing on the arm and leg were not what I was wearing that day. The picture shows brown shoes, blue jeans with a red jacket but I was wearing dark blue jeans tucked into beige knee-high boots with a loose knit brown top with a bright pink vest underneath. Now, we were looking at these pictures on a small digital camera so we couldn't see much more detail on the tiny screen, so we rushed back to the hotel to get a closer look on the laptop. We just couldn't work out what we were looking at...it was my head with someone else's body beneath it! And not only that, when you look closely you can see that it's actually the back of someone. Every little detail is there, the creases in the jeans the heel of the shoe, even a couple of fingers are visible. We didn't have a clue how it had happened and didn't immediately think it was a ghost as the details are so clear and the clothing is modern. We went through every single picture we took that day to see if there was anyone wearing those clothes, but there wasn't. I know there was no one near us when the picture was taken. It remains a mystery to this day so if anyone has an explanation as to how this could happen with a digital camera, I would love to hear it!

From Clare Gallagher

Hi Richard,

Please find attached the story of an incident I attended back in the nineties.

Intruder at the nursing home

This event took place some years ago yet remains vividly etched into my memory as the incident which revitalised my fascination with the paranormal.

I was a response Police Constable working in Maidstone, the county town of Kent in south east England. I was on night shift, crewed up with another PC who I shall call 'Scotty' owing to the fact that he was Scottish, and I like Star Trek.

He was a very dour man, did not suffer fools gladly but had a cynically dry sense of humour.

It was the early hours of the morning, I think around 3.00 am when we received an emergency call to a small residential nursing home in a village called Loose, located just outside of the town. The call had been made by a member of staff, who was reporting intruders on premises. The call dispatcher informed us that there had been loud banging on the exterior windows, as if someone was trying to break through the shutters, then the staff had heard someone actually walking around on an upper floor when they were all downstairs. It wasn't a resident as they were all elderly bed bound patients.

So, we arrived, adrenalin pumping, not knowing what to expect. The call dispatcher was still on the telephone to the home, usual practice for an intruder call, so we dashed straight in through the already opened main door. It struck me how utterly terrified the female nurse looked as she held the door for us. 'Where are we going?' I asked.

She pointed at a set of stairs in the main reception area. 'Up there.' Scotty and I drew our truncheons and torches and up we went. I recall it being quite a narrow staircase, single file only, with a couple of tight turns which prevented you from seeing around the corner. Upstairs, it was a very simple layout, just the one floor, turn left for one communal ward and right for another with built in storage cupboards in the middle. Basically, nowhere for anyone to go except past us. Fortunately, a dim light partially illuminated the landing which made our lives easier as we opened up every one of the cupboards to see if our intruder and tucked themselves away.

Anyway, the cupboards were clear, so now it was time to search the actual wards, where the lights were well and truly off. Scotty and I stood on the landing, peering into the darkness of the rooms, it seemed like every scrap of light had been sucked out. All the other response cars were dealing with other incidents, so it was just us. We agreed in hushed tones to take a ward each, but all I really wanted at that moment was to turn on every light and shout the usual warnings which in no uncertain terms urged the offender to give themselves up quietly. But, for the sake of the residents, who were elderly and quite poorly, that wasn't on the cards, so in we ventured.

I think the two things that unsettled me the most were seeing those blanket covered forms laying still on their beds and the noises that were coming from them. There were unintelligible mutterings, whimpering's, soft weeping, and even low chuckles. It wasn't their fault of course, my wife often tells me of the inhuman sounds I make in my sleep, but it was just so unnerving.

I searched under and around every bed and even double checked that there was only one occupant in each. Yes, some offenders have been known to hide in plain sight. At one point I remember standing up by a bed having just checked underneath and glancing at the person laying on it only to find them staring at me! I was about to open my mouth to whisper an apology but realised that they were actually still asleep, the chest moving up and down in that slow rhythmic manner of slumber.

Again, all clear, no intruders. I crept back out onto the landing and found Scotty was just emerging from his search. That was about the most I'd seen him so unnerved.

Having satisfied ourselves that there were no trespassers still on scene, we made our way back downstairs and found the staff room. There we found four absolutely terrified female members of staff. We quickly reassured them that the building was clear, then sent them off to see if anything was missing, while we checked around the outside of the premises. Reassuringly, all the windows and shutters were undamaged and totally secure. So, no evidence of any attempted forced entry and no intruder to be found. I must say that my curiosity was piqued, so we returned to the staff room where the four ladies were all back from their task. They informed us that there was nothing either damaged or missing anywhere in the building.
We all gathered in the staff room and were made a nice warm brew. They told us that it had been a busy night, one of the residents had sadly passed away earlier in the day and they had the job of sorting out their personal effects in addition to their usual tasks. Eventually, once things had settled, they all convened in the staff room for a well-deserved break. They were quite happily chatting away when everyone suddenly jumped out of their skins as three loud bangs rocked the shutters on the outside of one of two staff room windows. For a moment, the women were all a bit shocked and disorientated, but before they could do anything, there were three more loud bangs on the next window.

Thinking that someone was attempting to break down the shutters they collectively ran out of the room and into the reception area. No sooner had they done that, three more loud bangs came from one of the windows out there, immediately followed by bangs on the next window, then the next one. It was as if there was a person standing at each window of the building, taking turns to smash their fists against the shutters as hard as they could. Not getting any comfort from being in the foyer, they decided to retreat back to the staff room, another reason being that's where the only working telephone for night duty staff was located (no mobile phones back then). Really shaken now, they entered the staff room half expecting to see remains of glass and wood scattered on the floor. But there was nothing, all was intact and for a moment, everything went quiet.

Located on a wall in the staff room was a large intercom unit which they used to communicate with each other and monitor the wards upstairs. There was a matching unit on the upstairs landing and it was the usual practice of night staff to leave the intercom in the 'on' position in order that they could actually hear what was going on upstairs in the two wards. Apparently, the unit was super sensitive and could pick up any noise from either ward quite clearly. The ladies currently on duty were very adamant that by now, they could identify which sounds originated from the residents and the building.

So, back in the relatively safe confines of the staff room, the banging seemed to have stopped. They all stood round, on high alert, ready for the next crescendo. But instead of that, they all heard through the open intercom, the sound of heavy footsteps making their way across the upper landing. Very clear, distinctive footsteps. Not light, delicate or unsteady steps, but a determined steady tread. They looked at each other, stunned, clearly all realising simultaneously that there was nobody in the entire building, apart from the four of them who was remotely capable of walking up and down like that. Without exchanging a word, one of them just dashed to the telephone and rang 999. While the call was being made, the footsteps seemed to be heading from one side of the building to the other, it seemed to them that they then reached the location of the upper intercom, as if stood at the top of the staircase, just listening and waiting. Then all went quiet again and stayed quiet until they heard the noise of our police car.

Scotty and myself then spent some considerable time reassuring the ladies that no intruder remained on the premises and there was no physical evidence to suggest that there was one in the first place. There were differing lines of thought: two of the nurses were now definitely considering something supernatural. Another dismissed that entirely, based more on her religious beliefs than anything else. One was still too terrified to think anything and would more likely, not be back for another night shift.

We stayed as long as we could, but dawn was looming, and it was time to depart. As we were getting our gear together, two of the nurses took the opportunity to fetch some items from an under stairs cupboard back in reception. They had only been gone literally a minute when we heard piercing screams from outside the staff room. I shot out there and was confronted by two ashen faced nurses, both physically shaking. 'Footsteps.' one of them just about managed to say and pointed to the stairs 'Someone's going up there'.

I literally felt the adrenaline surge through my body and was instantly alert and pretty bloody angry at the audacity of this unknown person as I found myself bounding up the stairs in hot pursuit, not knowing or really caring if Scotty was behind me or not.

I expected to turn a corner on the staircase and be confronted by someone or something any second, I surely must have been right on their tail. But...nothing. I got to the upper floor and there was nobody in sight. There was absolutely no way that anyone could be that quick. Apart from the bed bound patients I was truly alone, so I did actually jump in the air as I heard quite clearly, the sound of heavy footsteps moving away from me, heading for one of the wards.

I was rooted to the spot. My career had been based around tangible, solid evidence, so standing there, listening to those footsteps was something pretty alien for me. Exercising the better part of valour, I didn't feel the need to continue the chase. My mouth agape I simply stayed as still as a statue until the footsteps seemed just to dissolve away. I made my way back downstairs in a bit of a trance and found Scotty was standing at the bottom, baton drawn, giving his best Scottish scowl.

Once again, we provided the requisite reassurance to the staff, but to be honest, I could have done with a bit myself. After a while we left to head back to the police station. En-route, our local control room radioed us requesting a result for the call. After a momentary hesitation I simply used the famous four words that any Copper will be familiar with. 'Area searched no trace.'

Apparently, nothing remotely paranormal had ever happened at the home before and as far as I'm aware, nothing happened after these events. Whether it was somehow connected to the resident who had recently passed, I couldn't say. Perhaps it was their way of saying goodbye and wanting to go out with a literal bang.

From Dave Elvy

Dear Richard

Now before I start this story let me tell you the lay out of the land around. This place is just outside Bolton in Farnworth. Hall Lane... The main road into Little Lever, on Hall Lane you have Moses Gate country park with Rock Hall and the river Croal and at the top of Hall Lane you have the Old Bury to Manchester canal as you walk along the canal you come to Ringley Locks and Nob End that has the old disused bell pits you can see today the ones that have sunk in .On Hall Lane itself you have a stone wall on one side of the road and remains of a stone building on the other side that you can still see when the weeds are cut back.

Now to the story

My brother lives in Little Lever and one day when I was 13, I was going to see him and my gran had asked me if I would take something round to him, I said ok and was just about to set off when she said these words watch out for the Hall Lane bugger? I asked what she meant and she said 'if you see him you will never forget him' and that was it to be honest I thought she was just trying to scare me as back then if it was going dark it was you better come in. By the time I had got to my brothers and back home I had forgot all about what my gran had said.

Now jump 2 years at 15, my brother had used my bike and I was on my way to his to pick it up and as I set off I saw an old friend of my grans heading to the country park and walked along with him he asked me where I was going and I said up Hall Lane to my brothers, his words where watch out for the Hall Lane Boggart

I said my gran said the Hall Lane bugger he then said well bugger or Boggart it's still the same so I asked him what is this Boggart and this is what he told me when he was a kid.

I was told this when I was a kid and my gran was told this by her mum as you know Hall Lane had houses on it and the story is one day a young lad set off to work in the pits he walked out of his house along the canal and down to Nob End, he had started work for the day but he never came home he was killed in a pit collapse.

My gran then told me that even though he had been killed many people had claimed to see him walking up or down Hall Lane or along the canal and that when people walked along Hall Lane in the dark it was like someone was behind you, you would turn round and no one there.

He told me this tale and I thought yep a tale to scare people and this is the last I had any thoughts about this tale till November 2019.

Flecky Bennett's Christmas ghost walk with a pub stop and at this pub you got a chance to talk about this walk with others on the tour. A guy on this tour asked me where I was from and I said just outside Bolton in Farnworth and he said that's a place I have not been in near on 50 years, he told me, his family had moved away when he was 10 and then said my dad used to tell me a tale about Farnworth the lane bugger, I said Hall Lane bugger and he said yes that's the one but he had never been told the whole story so I told him what I had been told and he was happy with the tale.

Now December the 29th 2019 and I was driving up Hall Lane and as I got to the top next to the turn in for the canal I see a young man stood at the side of the road not any young man but a man who you can see through it was day time and I slowed down as I went past I looked at him he had a flat cap on sunken eyes a dirty grey type shirt with rolled up sleeves black braces and brown pants and as I drove past I looked in the wing mirror and he had gone.

I have been along Hall Lane many times, walked the canal, walked around the locks and Nob End and never seen anything but like you Richard I feel the stone and water have something to do with ghost ......
This story is for my gran and goes back to, so it seems, from the early 1800s

From Carl Hodgson

Dear Richard,

My Dad told me a ghost encounter from about 40 years ago which he was so embarrassed about he only told it last year. He's a typical hard-working no-nonsense guy and he never usually tells anecdotes.

My Dad worked at the foundry in Milford and my parents bought a really old terrace cottage on Hopping Hill. Things in the house always went missing.

On one occasion he was working on something (can't remember what) and he dropped a key piece. He looked everywhere for weeks and it was never found. They had the room turned upside down. Other items in the house ended up in odd places with no logical explanation so something was going on.

One rainy day my Dad left the house and felt a presence following him, but there was nobody there. He got into his car and felt this presence in the back seat. Again, nobody there. He got to Allestree and the wipers on his car, which was always reliable, stopped. Quite annoyed and convinced something was in the back of the car, he got out of the driver's door, opened the rear door and said, "Come on you, OUT!" to a seemingly empty space. He got back into the car and the wipers started working again. From that day on. Nothing disappeared. Nothing moved. There was never an issue with the wipers on the car. He's convinced it was a spirit or a ghost.

From Stephen James

Hello Richard,

Back in May 2016, I awoke at 3.15 AM to go to the bathroom. I was on my own in the house as my wife was away, but otherwise everything was as normal. What was different, was that I opened the bedroom window blinds that night as I like to wake up with the sunrise, whereas my wife likes them closed.

Upon returning from the bathroom, I happened to look out and noticed my neighbours four-year-old daughter out in their garden. At 3.15 in the morning this seemed a bit unlikely, so I realised that I needed to take a closer look and be sure of what I was seeing. Clearly, she was sleepwalking, and had somehow managed to get outside of the house without waking her parents. I turned on the main bedroom lights and reached for my mobile phone.

Slightly unsure I went back to the window for a second look. There she was, standing at the end of the garden near the rear gate. It was at this point I noticed she was facing away and standing on a child's scooter, which had been left out from a busy day playing in the garden with the family. She had a short-bobbed haircut, dark hair and was wearing a long nightdress. She was standing with one foot on the scooter and the other on the floor to balance herself. It was a full moon that night, so whilst there was plenty of light, I couldn't tell the exact colour of the dress she was wearing, only that it was light in colour, probably white. I went back to the bathroom a second time and settled the dog, who had now also woken up early and wanted his breakfast.

I returned to the window a third time. Now fully awake and wondering what to do next, I could now clearly see that the child was holding on to the handlebars of her scooter and that she held her head forward and slightly to the side, swaying slightly, just as if she was fast asleep. I remember seeing her bobbed hair fall to the left as her head went from being upright to slumped down to the left. I watched her attempt to lift her floor standing leg and attempt to 'scoot' along but watched her quickly bring her foot back to the floor without successfully moving the scooter. I watched her repeat this at least three times before being startled by a black cat that jumped up onto the fence. The cat clearly and immediately noticed her as well in the garden, and cautiously aborted its attempt to jump down into the neighbour's garden, choosing instead to jump into ours.

Somewhere between five and ten minutes passed before I made the decision to alert the parents. The rear garden lead onto a road and this was potentially a dangerous situation for sleepwalking four-year-old. I scrolled down my contacts list and found my neighbours phone number, hesitated and then called them. It was 3.26 AM when I made the call according to my call history. He didn't answer, obviously.

I got dressed before taking one final look out of the window. She was still there, still on the scooter and still trying to move it. I went downstairs and round to my neighbour's front door and rang the bell. Both parents answered the door, startled and wearing dressing gowns. I told them, "so sorry to wake you but I've just seen your daughter in the garden, she looks like she's sleep walking!". Mum immediately ran upstairs whilst Dad half slammed the front door whilst frantically rushing for the back garden. I just went back inside and up to my bedroom window to see Dad retrieving the scooter and tidying the other garden toys left lying around. I then went back to bed feeling accomplished and quite proud that I'd avoided a potential situation.

The next day I saw Dad and apologised to him for waking them both up. I explained what I'd seen and that I thought it necessary to wake them. He replied "What on earth were you on about last night!!! She was fast asleep upstairs, and we have two child gates in place", "...and anyway she doesn't own a nightdress, only pyjamas. Plus, she's got long blond hair!". Of course, she wears pyjamas, whose children wear long white nightgowns in 2016! Startled and embarrassed, I could only apologise and explained that I must have been sleepwalking myself. But I know what I'd seen. I had triple checked that I wasn't daydreaming before acting. I was wide awake, completely conscious and can still recall every second of that experience.

The day after that I saw mum getting the kids into their car, who was rather more sympathetic and curious. She commented that their dog had strangely and unpredictably gone crazy earlier that same day, standing off and aggressively barking at the empty corner of the room. I saw their daughter who indeed had long blonde hair and was taller, which dismissed the idea that perhaps their daughter really was sleepwalking, and the parents were too embarrassed to admit it.

I still to this day can't explain the whole thing, but I know what I saw that night!

Mark from Mickleover, Derby.

Dear Richard
I have just seen your post requesting ghost stories/photos.
On Monday 1st March 2004, my daughter Charlotte and myself were in Leicester town center. We had been to a birthday party on the Saturday and had a "Boots" disposable single use camera that we were going to get developed.

We had two more photos to take so we took ourselves off to the Guildhall to use them up. It was a very bright, sunny day and nobody else was visiting at the time. I took one photograph in the library then we stepped outside onto the staircase overlooking the courtyard and took our final photograph. The camera was a single use disposable camera and I did not have a strap attached to it. We took the camera to Boots to be developed and picked it up an hour later.

All the photo's seemed normal. It was a few weeks later when looking at the courtyard photo that I noticed a shadow in the doorway, after zooming in with a magnifying glass I saw the figure in the doorway. I scanned the photo on my scanner so that I could look closer.

Just to confirm; when I took the photo there was nobody in the doorway. The figure, in relation to the height of the door would be about 3' tall.

I gave a copy of this photo to Derek Acorah who told me that the white misty anomaly in the photo is a "Vortex".

From Tracey Oakes

Dear Richard,

Quite a few years ago (either 2003 or 2004, I'm not 100% certain, I know it was September), myself and my aunt had travelled up to Norham Castle in Northumberland to watch a production by a local theatre group. The weather had been terrible all day, pouring down with rain, and obviously being open to the elements was doing no favours for the sound and lighting equipment.

After two hours of trying the engineers finally admitted defeat and cancelled the show. By the time we got back to our car it was around 10:30pm and we set off for home (Ashington). We had driven up the A697 on the way there and it seemed to take forever, so I decided to drive back home via the A1. We had just passed Haggerston Castle Holiday Park (between 2-5 miles south, at a guess) and were chatting away (probably grumbling about a wasted night!), and for a split second I saw what appeared to be a figure at the passenger window, like I say it was only there for a split second but it was definitely there.

I wasn't actually going to mention it because I wasn't 100% sure but when I looked across at my aunt she had a really puzzled look on her face, so I asked her, " Did you see that?" She said that she had and asked me what I saw. I told her that it looked like a figure standing looking through the window, with white around the head, and she said straight away, "It looked like a nun to me".

We spent the rest of the journey home trying to rationalise it, could it have been somebody standing at the side of the road? However, if that was the case, surely, I would have seen them in my headlights? But then again, the "figure" appeared centimeters from the passenger window, almost as if they were looking in, and was only there a split second. Also, I was driving at around 60mph, so nobody would've been able to get near my car at that speed. There are no bus stops or even footpaths in that area so there was absolutely no reason for anybody to be standing by the side of the road at that time of night.

Almost everyone I've told this story to has scoffed about it, but I remember that night as if it was yesterday and I know what I saw, and I fully believe it was paranormal.

Since that evening I have done a little bit of digging, but I admit to coming up with very little. The only piece of information that may be relevant is that Haggerston Castle was once used by the Poor Clare order of nuns in the late 18C. However, I can find no reports of nuns haunting the area.

Having lived in Northumberland my whole life until recently, and being very interested in ghosts and the paranormal, I consider myself to know a little bit about local ghost tales and folklore, but I knew absolutely nothing about reported ghost sightings on that particular stretch of road, until I bought a book by a local author, Darren W Ritson, who reported in his book "Haunted Northumberland" that there had been previous reports of apparitions on the A1.
Caley Sampson

Hi Richard,
It's Nicky.

Dear Richard,

I have a couple of stories. They both occurred at Derby Gaol in 2007 and 2008.

Firstly, I was setting up with the other Richard Felix Fans crew, for a Fan party in 2007. We were just setting up the food table, the music corner and karaoke table and busying ourselves in and out of the kitchen carrying trays and generally getting the party ready for the evening guests. The helpers were all getting into costume (it was one of the many costume parties that we used to have) I decided to get my silver Sony camera out and take a few shots of the action before the guests arrived, I was down the far end nearest the Condemned Cell, looking back up towards the bar end where the glass display cabinets were at and I took a photo of what was 2 of the female crew in costume walking passed the cabinets towards the food table in the seating area and thought nothing of it, we had a great evening all of us.

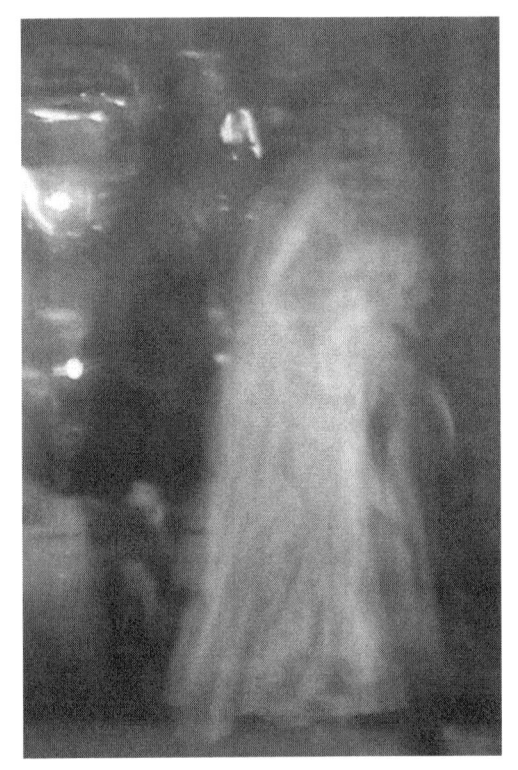

It was only when I uploaded the photos off my camera when I got back home to Birmingham, that I couldn't make out where the 2 girls were that should have been in the center of the photo, I had zoomed in too far I suppose in hindsight, but on closer appearance all I could see were many ghostly faces, 2 figures in the center which were indeed the 2 crew members but neither of them had faces, in fact the female on the left has Cavalier boots on when she was wearing a black dress and has a mans bearded head almost at her knee level and the white figure has her face superimposed with a young girls face that was not there at the time it was taken! There are a total of 5 ghostly heads and the pair of boots counted in the photo that should not have been there and were not visible to the naked eye! Spooky!

The second story I have was an overnight investigation with the Derby Gaol Paranormal Team back in 2008, it was the early hours of the morning when all the guests had gone home and the team were clearing up, putting everything back into place and generally having a sit down, relax and chat with a cup of tea before we locked up and went home.

There were 3 of us left in the Gaol, myself sat with a cup of coffee in the seating area nearest the bar and 2 other team members were in the Condemned cell packing up equipment, when I heard the kitchen tap running and cups or plates and cutlery being moved around as if being washed up! From where I was sat to the left of the fireplace, I couldn't see who had walked past me to the kitchen to do the washing up but I thought it strange they hadn't put the light on behind the bar so they could see what they were doing, so I called out, "how can you see what you are doing in there, and who does the washing up at 3am anyway?" .... only to be met by 2 voices coming from the Condemned Cell calling up to me saying "who are you talking to Nicky?"!

Well my response was "If you are both down there, who is washing up in the kitchen?" .... I felt my heart beat out of my chest somewhat as I stood up and crept around the corner to see if I could see who was in fact washing the crocks up, as the light wasn't on behind the bar I leant around to switch it on from the front side hearing the crocks being swilled in the kitchen still ..... as I switched it on, the clatter stopped abruptly, and it was silent.

By this time the two team members had met me at the front side of the bar area as confused as I was, we all walked around the bar side together into the bright strip lighted kitchen, to see all the cups, plates and cutlery all neatly stacked as it had been left earlier in the night and the kitchen sink was bone dry, not even a drip from the tap!

To this day, I have no idea why a ghost would want to be washing up at 3am but I am grateful they didn't start clattering around whilst I was making my coffee in there 20 minutes beforehand!!

The strangest experiences I have ever had Richard, and they were both in your Gaol. I cannot fathom out either of them or I probably never will now.

I shared the second experience with Chris and Eleanor and it was both of them in the Condemned Cell that night, and we decided it must have been a recording of a scene that happened long ago, stone tape theory springs to mind!

From Nicky Roberts was McArdle

Hi Richard

I was brought up in Leeds and have lived here all my life. Our family home was in Beeston, south Leeds. The next town along was Middleton. We were connected to Middleton by a huge wood by the same name. Middleton woods and the land they are a part of has lots of ghost stories. I'm sure not all of them are true. I'm sure most of them are stories that kids tell to spook each other. But one thing that is true is that Middleton woods, Middleton lodge and surrounding areas used to be owned by the Maude family, a very wealthy family around the 1800s. Middleton lodge, I believe was built in 1760. Unfortunately, no longer standing. Middleton also had a coal mine that went under the woods. As a kid, I used to play in the sink holes that had been created from when the mines were running years earlier. I'm sure there are many secrets in the woods as it has had so much activity over the years.

My story took place in 1989. I'm a typical 16 year old. My two close friends and I had discovered that we can get served alcohol in our local shop so quite often would pop to the shop and buy a couple of cans each on a Friday night. We could never get served in the pub due to one friend looking very young and other than drink beer, there was nothing for teenagers to do.

Anyway, we would pop to the shop, buy our beer and head to Middleton woods where we wouldn't be seen drinking beer on the streets. I'm sure we would have looked like yobs and our parents (whom were all respectable people) would have gone crazy. So, we headed to the woods where we could have a drink and chat about the things that 16yo lads talk about. Let me just add at this point, we were actually pretty good kids and were NOT yobs. Never smoked or took drugs.

We always took the same route while walking in the woods. We used to walk along an old tram line that closed down some thirty years earlier and was mostly grown over. Then we used to drop down to a single track that had been formed in the undergrowth. There were many dirt tracks and walkways probably formed by dogs and walkers alike over the years. As we continued our walk along this very narrow track, we noticed it was getting darker so decided to head back home. We walked in single file as the track wasn't wide at all. Garry was in front. Then me and finally Paul who always seemed to have his head elsewhere. Not saying he wasn't intelligent or anything. He was actually a very bright kid but always seemed pre-occupied. Never seemed to be on the same page as anyone else. So, Garry and I were chatting while walking along the single path while Paul seemed to just tag along behind.

Then, there it was. But what exactly was "it?". Well, it just appeared from nowhere. A white mass. That's probably the best way to describe it. A white mass about 4ft wide and 2ft high. No particular shape to it either. It was just a blob. And it just appeared from nowhere. It didn't fly or climb or walk or run. It just appeared and was there. It moved as well. Not like moved around or went anywhere but when I say moved, I mean it was just moving. Like if you nudge a jelly on a plate and watch it wobble. It wasn't solid either. We could see through it, but it wasn't clear like glass. More like it was obscure. Like a milky white. A white mass that appears from nowhere and has motion to it. We can see through it but not clearly. The edges of it seemed more transparent than the main body (if that's what you can call it).

And then gone. As quick as it appeared, it vanished. Not like a light switching off but more like it faded into nowhere. All this happened within just a second or two from appearing to vanishing. Garry had stopped dead in his tracks and swung his head round at me. I stopped walking too. Paul didn't. He walked into the back of me. Garry's face was pale. He asked me, "Did you see that?" I tried to respond. I tried to say yes, I saw it. My mouth opened but no words came out. I was happy in once sense that what I knew I had seen had just been confirmed by Garry. But in the other sense I was absolutely petrified that the confirmation from my friend must have meant that we just saw a ghost.

We all ran. Even Paul. We ran till we left the woods and into the safety of the streets in our neighbourhood. Once in the streets under a streetlamp, Paul asked, "What was it?" We thought he was asking what we all saw and both Garry and myself together with no prompting said, "We just saw a ghost." Paul was NOT impressed. He actually didn't see it. He actually thought we were pranking him. He told us how he couldn't believe we made him run like that.

Weeks went by and Paul still didn't believe that what we saw was real. He told other friends who of course took the mick. People started throwing in suggestions as to what they thought we saw. Suggestions like, it could have been a carrier bag floating in the wind or a pigeon or car headlamps. A cat climbing a tree perhaps. Even fog. We've heard them all. We would tell them. "This thing appeared from nowhere." First it wasn't there. Then it was. Then it wasn't. I watched it vanish like captain Kirk beaming back up to the enterprise. It didn't run off or float away in the wind or switch off. I didn't climb up or down the tree. It just............... went.

Thirty years later and we still chat about it. Only now we chat to our kids about it. Paul has accepted that Garry and I did see something but still refuses to believe it was a ghost. He is still to come up with an explanation.

From Mark Richards.

Hi I'm Peter Sugden

For my sins I'm a Ghost Hunter, when you tell people what you do, they inevitably always ask a lot of questions, but two questions specifically.

The first one is "Have you ever seen a ghost?" well I am afraid the answer to that is you'll have to read my book about it The Adventures of a Ghost Hunter - available on Amazon in paperback or kindle formats. I know it's a cheap plug - sorry about that :-)

The second question I'm so often asked is "Why do I believe in the paranormal?" well to answer that question I have to tell you a little bit about my family and in particular

The Haunted Bell -

At the end or near the end of my Great Aunt's life - she came to stay here with us my mother and myself basically end of life care really , she had a very good few months with us but unfortunately after about 8 months she did actually pass .

Now my aunt used to have the spare room upstairs and whenever she needed my mother to help her with food or whatever she would ring a bell. Mum would tend to her every need I think my aunt enjoyed the fuss

It's an antique bell, a cast iron hand bell. I have no idea where it came from just something Aunty Ginny had. Now she would ring this bell all times day and night we got accustomed to it Towards the end of her life she slipped into an unconscious state and was taken to the hospital, the prognosis well was not good, and as this was late in the evening we all decided to go to the hospital next morning to be with her and with that we had to try and get some sleep knowing she was near death

I was awoken suddenly at exactly 02.43 am the bell was ringing persistently and quite loudly. I looked at my clock, my electric clock and it said 02.43 am

in actual fact it had stopped that very moment at 02.43 and it never worked again it couldn't have been the batteries because had the batteries failed I wouldn't have been able to see the luminous light telling the time , it had just stopped

I called my mother because of the bell but she didn't hear me and didn't answer then of course I realized that my aunty wasn't there this was quite disturbing I was still quite young at the time I went back to bed again loosely slept until the phone rang waking us at 08.00 am it was the nursing sister from the hospital

She told us that my aunty had passed away peacefully in her sleep at 02.43 am coincidences in this case I cannot accept because it was too exact but not really surprising when you think who my aunty really was

I knew her all my life as Aunty Ginny she was my grandfather's sister a kind lady who cared for us dearly. She was a celebrated person in her own tight in the world of spiritualists and spiritualist movement but of course in 30's 40's and 50's this was definitely frowned upon.

oh no this was; well taboo really within the church and the family they didn't want to be associated with it particularly my grandfather a lovely man in every way but was set in his ways. He would not have any conversation about it

Her name was Emma Jane Ratcliff and she was in her own right a celebrated spiritualist.

pictured here with my Granddad

She had "Visions" which usually came to her in her sleep , she saw a young boy walk into the road and get knocked down by either a lorry or a bus (I say this because different members if the family remember this story slightly differently) what was remarkable was that this was an American child . Although my great aunt had never left the Manchester area in her life, let alone been out of the country she could not possibly have known an American family or even their child or where they lived but she also saw in her vision their name and their address. She wrote a letter unbeknown to her family to this American family explaining who she was that she'd had a vision moreover she was seriously concerned for the child in particular and that there was still time to prevent any harm coming to him she wrote this letter and it was received by the family I'm not sure whether they believed my aunty or they thought this letter was a crank but nevertheless the little boy did wonder out into the street and the parents pulled him back just before he would have been run over by a lorry or a bus. The lady the American was distraught and on her own reflection felt the need that she had to thank my aunty for the information aunty had given her. She wrote a beautiful letter to my aunty saying how grateful she was the letter unfortunately has been lost in tine I have been trying to find it through family members but we have not found it Yet

To think that she did this long before I was born and this was the story that was passed through the family of course but not through my grandfather because he would not have tolerated it but it's these two things these two stories about such a great lady that bring me to tell you now the answer to the question "Why do I believe in the paranormal?"

You see I cannot prove or disprove the paranormal world, nobody can but I believe there is something too it because I cannot deny the evidence of my own experience.

Peter Sugden

Hi, my name is Karen Oliver, I live in Sheerness in Kent.
I have many ghost story's since being a child. He's 3 of my favourites

My first is of a horse that haunts Glen Wood drive, Minster Sheppey Kent.

One boiling hot summers day in the late 1980s enjoying a family afternoon in my auntie's garden, 7 of us in the garden surrounded by 8ft fencing heard the clip clop of horses hooves coming down the road, not unusual because there are stables nearby, the hooves got louder as they approached, we all rushed to peep holes in the fence to see the horse, but instead of seeing a horse we heard a horse rearing up so loud, there was no horse to be seen, no more sound of hooves. The story goes that a young girl got killed on her horse there in the 1960s.

Dancing Dolly Hill Minster Sheppey Kent. A small alleyway runs from minster Abbey behind an old pub, a regularly used alley. In the early 1980s my aunty was walking down the alley after dropping my cousin off at playschool, she heard a rustling behind her looked back, nothing, a few moments later rustling again, she looked back and there was a nun floating down behind her, my aunty quickly dashed and crossed the road into the butchers shop, the butcher knew what my aunty was going to say, the nun walked through his shop every morning, story goes there was a Nunnery somewhere behind where the old butchers shop stood back in the 1300/1400s.

The old man at halfway cemetery, when I was around 5yrs old I visited the cemetery with my mum, I kept hearing rustling behind us as we walked, I looked behind and a man was following us, brown pin stripe trousers, white shirt, braces, bowler hat, pipe, walking stick, he seemed to be getting closer and closer, twice I said mum look, twice my mum couldn't see this man. In the end to pacify me she said he's probably bent down to a grave, 10yrs later while visiting my aunty she was telling ghost stories, she told the story of the old man that sits on the halfway cemetery wall, smoking his pipe, swinging his legs in his brown pin stripe suit, well I looked at my mum, my mum looked at me gob smacked, I'd seen him that day as clear as anything.

From Karen

Hi Richard

Back in the late 70's we lived in a house that was haunted by a young man. This young man (I believe was in his 20's) lived in the house before my parents moved there in 1977, he believed his mother was a witch and she practiced Black magic, he got it in his head that black magic would save him if he tried to kill himself so he decided to hang himself on some exposed pipes in one of the bedrooms. Obviously the hanging did kill him and he was found by his mother when returning to the house, she was very distressed by what she found and decided she was going to move house and the next people who was going to live in the house was going be haunted by her son by putting a curse on the house.

My parents, sister and I, I was only 3 years of age at the time, and my sister was a baby, moved into this house which by the way was in Hull. We started to experience various things now obviously I was too young to remember much, all this I'm telling you is what my parents have told me, but he was a noisy ghost and I can remember been awoken by him one Christmas and my mum convincing me that it was father Christmas on our roof coming to our house which obviously got me straight back to sleep.

A few experiences my parents told me about was hearing him walking up and down our stairs, my dad was in bed for 6 weeks with Yellow jaundice and often heard him walking around the house. My auntie once visited our house and my mum opened the front door and saw this spirit walking down our stairs, she ran back out again never to return.

My Nanna was once there and she was doing her makeup, she was sat on our leather sofa putting lipstick on, looking in a small vanity mirror and out of the corner of her eye she noticed the cushion on the sofa had gone down as if someone was sat there but no-one was and my Nanna calmly said' none today thanks' and she saw the cushion rise again as if someone had stood up again.

I used to have a big toy snail that was at the end of my bed and this spirit used to come and sit on the snail and talk to me and read me stories but when either my mum or dad come in to see who I was talking to there was no one there, my parents slowly had enough and finally moved house in 1980.

My mum saw her ex next door neighbour some months later and asked if anyone had moved into our old house the neighbour said yes, mum asked and is the ghost still there and the neighbour said no it's gone completely quiet after talking to the new occupants, so it looked like the black magic curse put on by the witch was true we were the only ones to be haunted by her dead son!

From Neil Till

Dear Richard,
here's our story about a ghost sighting in Mansfield.
Several years ago, we were working at a local music bar, Fat Sam's. It was lunch time and myself, my husband, my son, Sam and Steve were having coffee in the front lounge.

A man walked past the front window. We didn't think anything of it at first, but then the doors moved as they did when anyone came in due to the air pressure. As we were closed, one of the men went to inform the person. There was no one there! A quick search was done in case the man had gone upstairs or into the main room. My son also went outside to see if he could see the man, but there was no one.

I later related this incident to my father. When I described the man, he said it sounded like Mr. Fowler. He said this man had run a ping pong hall just around the corner from the club and his house had been where the club's stage now was.

The man always went home for his dinner every day, and yes, he was dead. We realised that the doors often banged in the same way at the same time, and people had said they thought someone had entered the building.

We all saw the man pass the window, and he looked "real", wearing a dark trilby, dark overcoat, with a cigarette in the corner of his mouth.

From Cheryl

Hello Richard,

Here's a ghost story that actually happened to me when I was ten and till this day I still can't explain.

When I was 4-5, my great aunt who I was very close to and saw a lot, died of cancer, I've been told by relatives that in her latter days, the cancer had got hold of her and she was constantly asleep, however when I came into the room, she would sit up for me and smile. Then she had to go to hospital, and I gave her a teddy bear, the day before she died, she gave me the teddy back with a little one sewn onto it. (she loved sewing) this I still have.

Fast forward 5 years, I'm ten years old and I have these strange, recurring dreams where my room would be pitch black and I could see and sense it was her. Her eyes were like the headlamps on cars. She said repeatedly don't open the mirror your too young. Then the dream abruptly ended. I would have this dream for about 2 times a week for a while on and off.

One day about two months after it started, I had an arts and crafts room but wasn't allowed to go in alone god forbid I were to break something. But one day I had a peculiar urge to walk in there as little kids do. So, I did. I found a lovely pocket mirror with a cross stitch pattern in there and whilst admiring it, it slipped and dropped out of my hand and hence smashed. Around the same time the dreams stopped. I thought it was because my mum put the teddies into storage that she gave me but when I was older, I realised that was my aunts mirror and when I got the teddy out of storage, the dreams didn't come back. So, I think it was the mirror and the dreams have never come again. It is still a mystery about what the dreams were about and still will be.

From CT.

Hi Richard,

I thought you might be interested in this (true) ghost story involving a cat. I'm not sure how common animal ghost stories are but here's ours.

We owned a black and white cat called Archie. At 2 years old he had what I would call a charmed life. At night he'd be allowed out to roam and my wife, Julia, would get up early (ish) in the morning, rattle the keys at the back door and he'd come running in, up the stairs, across the wood floor in our bedroom and go to sleep at the bottom of our bed. So this particular morning was no different, I was sitting up in bed and heard him run up the stairs, cross the wood floor, he wasn't a small cat and so the noise was considerable, except he went under the bed. My wife came up and told me "the cat hasn't come in yet get ya cloths on" and went off before I could tell her he's under the bed. I looked but couldn't find him under there. So, we went out the back where there's a long, grassy verge bordered by high bushes and trees but couldn't see him. On the other side of the trees is a main road. We found Archie lying dead at the side of the road. The sound of him coming in and running up the stairs and across the wood floor will stay with me for the rest of my life and really made me think about the possibility of something else after we die. I have no photos to offer just a heartfelt ghost story.

From Barry Taylor

Hi Richard

I was one doing a nighttime patrol of the hospital and was walking back to security office it was approx. 02:30 and I saw a doctor in a white coat he was really old, and I did not recognise him as staff I said, 'hi are you well' and he did not reply and walked past me. I turned round to see him walk straight though a locked door to a department that was closed at night. I went to check the area and the door was locked and no lights on etc. I radioed up my work mate and he checked the cctv and said I was the only person on the corridor at the time.

I have also heard screaming for help next to a lift shaft in the nurses' tower block. I later found out that a nurse had jumped down the lift shaft committing suicide, as she was finding work and hours too much, but this was not talked about much.

From Richard Barber

Dear Richard,

My father Gunnar Romer was a builder who built a bungalow stands in the grounds of what was once the site of St. Saviour's Hospice, a site long centuries gone. When building the bungalow's extensive cellars out, this was 1963 and the Cuban Missile Crisis led him to build a bunker under his house, he unearthed many human skeletons.

He called the police, and of course the Coroner was notified. The skeletons were found to be medieval and related to the Hospice.

The builder did not scare easily. Someone was stealing his bricks and building materials overnight, so he put the bodies to good use, affixing the skulls to posts where they leered evilly at the would-be thief. At night he would put candles in them on the posts, and the unfortunate thief did himself an injury running away screaming in the dark.

When he had finished, he reburied them in accordance with the Coroner's instructions. I suppose many people will feel he was asking to be haunted!

One night while sitting in the kitchen he saw a figure through the frosted glass of the kitchen doorway, wearing a light brown mackintosh. He called "come in Ted" assuming it to be Ted Bentley his father in law. There was no response, so he called out again. Still the visitor did not come in. "Come in you silly old fool" he yelled and wandered over to the door through which the figure remained visible, throwing it open and finding no one there. There was no way someone could have run off and he could find no optical effect to explain it away. Did he see the ghost of a monk?

The bungalow had a series of weird manifestations of the poltergeist type and the nearby Abbeyford garage is reputedly haunted too. One cleaner quit after seeing the clocks run backward!

From Chris Jenson Romer

Hi Richard,

Three ghosts have been seen in the grounds of the 400-year-old Bispham Hall in Billinge, Lancashire.

Most frequently seen, in the month of August, is a lady dressed in white flowing robes who walks 200 yards from the house to an ornamental lake.

A man dressed in riding habit has been seen standing near a clearing. He vanishes into thin air when approached.

The spirit of a dog sits close to a little grave. On the gravestone is the inscription 'Alas Poor Faithful'. In the 1970s, a white dog was seen near the grave in daylight.

Our group investigated the Hall while it was under construction in 1995/96. When Edwin Fisher took a picture of the first-floor corridor (19 November 1995) there was a bang on the master bedroom door. The incident was recorded on a camcorder.

Our group investigated Wycoller Hall in 1995/96. There were reports of unexplained sounds where the scullery used to be.

On 21 July 1995, we heard a woman humming the Disney song 'When You Wish Upon A Star'. The sound occurred again an hour later but at a fainter level. The woman hummed the song an hour after that but was barely audible. Five members of our group (Peter Crawley, Martin and Paula Roscoe, Edwin Fisher and Colin Veacock) recorded a sound similar to a riding crop on 26 July 1996.

From Peter Crawly

Dear Richard,

A few years ago, I was working as a Security Officer on a fire station in South Wales, unfortunately I can't name it as it is still in use. My very first shift there was a Saturday morning. I arrived half an hour or so before my shift started so that my colleague who had worked the nightshift prior, could show me around. I did the handover with him and settled into my shift. I should point out here that this fire station, at this time, was a retained station meaning that the firefighters not stationed there like a full-time station but were called in for a shout by the means of an pager.
We, the security staff, were stationed on the 1st floor in the mess room. Around an hour into my shift I heard the main door slam and footsteps on the stairs, one of the firefighters had come into the station to collect some belongings. His words when he saw me "Alright mate? You're one of the security guards, are you? Have you seen the ghosts yet?" I just laughed and had a quick conversation with him,

dismissing his comment about the ghosts as I knew only too well that firefighters have a reputation for pranks, he soon left the station and I settled back down to my duties. A short while later another firefighter came to the station, coming into the mess he saw me and said "Hi mate, Security yeah? Have you seen the ghosts yet?" My response was, to myself, this has to be a joke and they're all in on it. I just replied jokingly. "Yes, mate have you got the number for the Ghostbusters?" His reply shook me, without even a flicker of a smile he replied." No mate this place is bloody haunted." He did what he had to do and left, leaving me pondering his reply even though I was on my toes for a prank something told me there was an element of truth in what I was being told.

I tried to put it to the back of my mind, but when I was carrying out a patrol I saw, from a 1st floor window a car, pull on to the forecourt. A man wearing a white shirt with black epaulettes with white pips on, indicating he held a high rank, got out and walked to the station. Immediately I thought to myself I am going to get some answers, I ran down the stairs meeting him outside the watch room. Exactly, the same, as the others his response to seeing me was the same including asking if I had seen the ghosts. I then asked him out right if this was true and not some joke to wind up the security staff. His response was." This station is haunted to buggery mate; if I didn't have to be somewhere, I'd stay and tell you. But yes, this place is haunted you'll soon find out.". I was taken aback by this, but I let him carry on with what he had to do and carried on with my patrol of the station.

Towards late afternoon/early evening, the first firefighter I had met that day arrived back at the station, I saw him arrive from a 1st floor window. I was determined now to get some answers I went into the mess room and put the kettle on as he walked into the room I offered him a cup of tea, he accepted my offer, once he had done what he had to do. When we were both sat around the table, I asked him what had been happening, please bear in mind these events had happened over a number of years. This is what he told me. In 1878 on the site of the now fire station, stood a colliery on September 11th an explosion ripped through the mine trapping 325 men and boys below ground. Despite a valiant effort by the rescue team, 268 men and boys were killed or trapped in parts of the mine by the explosion, with fear of more explosions the local government and the mine management diverted water from the local canal flooding the pit. When they began salvage work to re-open the pit in 1882 bodies and parts of bodies were found scattered throughout the mine, it is believed many of the miners were trapped and not killed by the explosion but dying from drowning.

The fire station now stands on the site of the old pit head. The station was once full time and then went to a day manning system, where Monday to Friday it was manned between 9am & 6pm after these hours and on the week end it was retained. A new firefighter started there when it was day manning, he travelled from Swansea, a fair distance away, to save travelling back and forth each day he sought permission from the senior officers to sleep on station between his duties, they agreed and gave him a bed in one of the disused offices. On his first night staying there he went to bed around 10pm and fell asleep, during the night he heard knocking on the office door he called out "Come in" thinking a fellow firefighter had returned to the station, no one came through the door. He shrugged thinking it was a dream, a couple of minutes later more knocking came from the office door he leapt out of bed throwing open the door, finding the corridor empty. He threw on some clothes and searched the entire station, he found no one else there. Returning to the office he was thinking to himself that it must have all been a very vivid dream, he had just closed the door when more knocking came from the other side he opened it again rather angrily and found nothing. Not wasting anymore time he grabbed his belongings and bedding spending the rest of the night in the car. After this incident he bought a camper van while stationed here vowing never to spend another night in the station again.

Years after this the station became retained. One afternoon a senior officer had come into the station to do some paperwork, he was sat in the watch room hearing a squeal of tyres he looked through the window into the rear yard and saw a fellow firefighter getting out his car with his wife both were having a blazing row. The senior officer, not wishing to be involved in a domestic carried on with his work, suddenly he heard a scream coming from the rear yard, thinking the other fire fighter had attacked his wife, he ran out into the yard finding the wife sobbing hysterically on the floor her husband trying to comfort but looking confused as he had no idea what had caused this. They brought her, still sobbing into the watch room after calming her down they asked her what happened to cause her to go into hysterics. She told them that as she and her husband were arguing she looked past him up into one of the 1st floor windows where she saw the shape of a head there, which suddenly vanished. Both men checked the whole station, finding no- one else in the station.

The firefighter continued telling me about the hauntings, in the middle of the night the crews on call have been alerted to a call and raced to the station where they've found all the lights on right through the building and doors open, again with no-one in the building. With most retained stations, after a call the crew will gather in the station to have a cup of tea and a chat, but at this station at night the crews just get back and go home none of them will stay in the station, after dark, any longer than they have to. When there are adverse weather conditions forecast, i.e. heavy ice or snow, the on call crew will be called by fire control at home and requested to head to the station to answer any calls, the reason being is to save any of them crashing on- route to the station. They will all sleep in the same room where they've heard doors slamming elsewhere in the station and then they will all be arguing as to who goes and investigates the noises however none of them will. This struck me as strange as firefighters are willing to run into burning buildings to save people, yet they will not go round their own station at night.

As I previously mentioned I have a deep interest in the paranormal and listened to him with interest, when my colleague who came back in that night I told him everything but he played it all down and said flatly that ghosts do not exist and it was all a joke. A few days later I arrived around 6.30am for my 7.00am start, my colleague was stood outside the front door of the station, I hadn't even switched the engine off on my car, he had my door open saying something had happened he was talking rapidly, so much so I had to ask him to slow down so I could understand what he was saying. Sometime during the small hours, he was looking out of the window behind him he saw 3 figures, " Looking like miners walking across the room." This was followed by several doors banging through the station. I said to him that I thought he didn't believe in ghosts his reply was that he had strongly changed his mind after that night duty. On another duty I was upstairs in the mess room I finished a cup of coffee and conducted a patrol of the station, I was shocked to find all the lights on in the appliance bay, and all the doors to the appliances were wide open. I knew the lights were off and the appliance doors were closed from my previous patrol and hour or so previously. Another occasion I was conducting a patrol on the ground floor I heard doors being slammed upstairs, I ran upstairs again finding nothing.

I was speaking to a friend of mine one afternoon on the phone he too holds an interest on the paranormal, I was explaining to him everything that I had been told and everything that I had experienced at the station. During this conversation with him I saw, out of the corner of my eye a figure walking towards the door I spun round immediately finding the room empty. Working there was an experience that I'll never forget.

From Dorian

Hi Richard,

Don't know whether you would be interested in something that happened to me that I've never spoken about in years, for fear of being thought bonkers, unhinged or something, which I'm pretty certain I'm not.

In 1976 I started my nurse training at the old Pendlebury children's hospital on Manchester Road Pendlebury. During this time, I often used the post office amongst the couple of other shops near to the hospital as it was convenient.

I don't know the exact year, but I think it was sometime around 1978, it was the spring of that year around April time, I think. I was invited to a friend's 21st birthday party. I accepted and was looking forward to the event which was to be held in Accrington my friend's hometown. Due to work commitments I totally forgot to make a hair appointment with my usual hairdresser. When I attempted to make the appointment, I couldn't get in anywhere. I was about to give up and go back to my room in the nurses residence and do my own hair. When on my way back I passed the small row of shops where the post office was. I chanced to glance up at th bay window above the post office and saw a hairdryer (the type you sat under).

At the time I thought it looked a bit old fashioned, but I thought well, I will try and get in for a blow dry.

I noticed a side door, went in, and had to climb a staircase which would have been more at home in a stately home than leading to a hairdressers shop. I reached the top of the stairs which opened into the hairdressers, it was only small, and there was no one in but a middle-aged lady who was quite attractive if not a little dated. She had fair hair to her shoulders and a wraparound overall on in a floral print. I remember her long scarlet painted nails, in an era when everything was the natural look.

I asked if she could do my hair and she said certainly what did I want? I said a blow wave and she looked at me really oddly, she said leave it to me I know exactly what will suit you. She then proceeded to put rollers in my hair, which horrified me. I was too polite as a youngster to disagree, so sat through it. When she had finished, she seemed thrilled and was showing me the end result with the mirror from all sides. I was mortified and was more bothered about having to walk back to the nurse's residences with this dreadful hair disaster that looked like it was from the ark.
When I attempted to pay, she just waved me away and said enjoy the party and happy birthday to your friend.

I got back to my room and promptly wet my hair and did what I could with it before setting off to the party. I was getting a lift with other friends.

I never thought anymore of it, until maybe 3 months or so later when I was talking to the man who was behind the counter in the post office. I mentioned having my hair done in the hairdressers upstairs. What had struck me was the back door was open the room was full of cardboard boxes, the stair case was there but it was nowhere near in the pristine condition it was when I climbed it to go to get my hair done.

I said, "does the lady use the side entrance?" He looked at me oddly and said, "I'm sorry, what do you mean". So, I said "the hairdresser upstairs, does she use the side entrance as the stairs are blocked with boxes". He said, "there's nothing upstairs, it's an overflow storeroom come stock area". He said we rarely ever go up there. By now I was feeling a bit odd, because I'd realised that the stairs looked so unkempt to what I had witnessed. I didn't say anymore to the post office clerk, I thought he would think me strange so never followed it up.

I started back to the nurse's residence and an idea suddenly struck me, so I retraced my steps and went to look for the entrance door on the side of the building at the foot of the stairs. Now, this is the weirdest thing EVER, and prompted me never to mention what happened to me until now, there was NO DOOR. There was no evidence that there had ever been a door, in the brick work. I hastily left. I never mentioned it and it troubled me every time I walked past, I couldn't help glancing at that bay window above the post office, it was just full of stacked boxes. No hairdryer no evidence of a hairdresser. I have looked into it but have not come up with an explanation. Sometimes I wonder if I dreamt it, but on another level, I know I didn't. I have a photograph taken at the 21st birthday and it always makes me feel creepy when I see it.

It's not a ghost story as such. Call it time slip, I don't know. Some things we can't explain and never will. Maybe we are not meant to.

From Julie Hayes

Dear Richard,

It's not actually my story, this happened to my uncle, but I ask him to retell it every time I see him because it fascinated me so much.

This happened about 20 years ago and at the time my aunt and uncle were living in a big thatched cottage in a village in Buckinghamshire. I'm a bit reluctant to name exactly where in case the people living there now read this! It was (and still is) a lovely building, absolutely steeped in history, and as a big history fan I used to really love visiting them and looking in all the nooks and crannies of the place and soaking up the atmosphere. They lived there from when I was a toddler to when I was in my early twenties, so I had lots of opportunities over the years to have a good nose about! I remember the massively crooked floors upstairs, small windows and big thatched roof, and the strange, dark feeling at one end of the property and the general feeling of being watched. The building dated from the early 17th century and I think was originally two weaver's cottages that had been knocked into one. Strange things had happened over the years but nothing too noticeable, such as the water being turned off at the mains and the video recorder starting by itself, that sort of thing. It was surprising to me that not more had happened, because the building really was very atmospheric.

Then twenty years ago, my aunt and uncle were going out somewhere and as they walked down the path to the car, my uncle realised he'd left the car keys on the dining table, so he nipped back inside to grab them. As he stepped into the dining room to grab the keys, he happened to look up through the kitchen door and was stunned to see a lady standing there by the sink, looking back at him. He described her in great detail, and said she was wearing a long dark dress with an apron and a 'sort of pointed hat' or cap. My uncle is not interested in history at all, so he would've been clueless about the sort of clothes people would have worn in the past, or at least he wouldn't really have been aware of the details. But her outfit as he described it matches perfectly with the clothes that would have been worn by weavers at around the time the cottage was built.

The thing which fascinated me when he first told the story and still fascinates me now is that he said that when he looked at her, she was looking back at him and they made eye contact, and she looked just as shocked to see him as he was to see her. I'm fascinated by the idea of time slips and of time overlapping, perhaps this was one of those cases?

Anyway, he didn't hang about, he grabbed the keys, left the cottage, and went on his way, and even though I make him retell the story he doesn't like talking about it, it really scared him. I do know he's said he wasn't really thinking about anything when he went to collect the keys, and from the hundreds of ghost stories I've read over the years, that usually seems to be the case.

From Sammy

Hello Richard,

Me and my partner frequently visit York for its history, tales and of course pubs! We have stayed in the Guy Fawkes Inn 3 times. We have had two STRANGE encounters in that building the 1st stay and the 3rd and last stay, as my partner will no longer stay there because of this. We also had a strange encounter in The Golden Fleece.

On the first stay, I remember walking into my room (on the top floor) and it felt lovely, 4 poster bed, old furniture, and a real lovely atmosphere. We went out that night had a few drinks and came back for a good night's sleep as normal around 11pm. About 4am in the morning my partner woke me up by firmly clutching my whole body and pointed at the chandelier that was on the ceiling swinging. Not just a faint gust of wind swing. Almost like a pendulum swinging, with the sound of rattling coming from the crystals or whatever it was on it. Being sceptical I checked all the windows to ensure they were closed and not letting in any wind or draught, they were (being a winters night). I thought maybe someone on the upper floor was moving around a lot. I opened my room door to find there was no upper floor. The chandelier continued to swing at quite a rate for around 2-5 minutes. It's hard to say exactly being petrified at the time as well as sceptical. It's safe to say after 3 years of thinking about it, it certainly spooked us both.

On the second stay, me, and my partner again, went out for a few drinks came back around usual time 11-12pm and went to sleep. The door was opposite our bed with the light shining under the door from the landing. It's probably worth mentioning that because of the age of the building there was an unevenness to the floor, so a lot of light was coming through under the door. This is important! Also, our room was right at the top of the stairs.

My partner awoke me around 2am and said the sound of someone walking upstairs had woken her (which is normal as the stairs were old and creaky) and some black boots had walked in front of our door and stopped. We could see the black boots on the landing under our room door. I assumed it was someone coming upstairs and maybe checking his phone or finding his keys?
But there was no noise or movement, and this lasted around a minute. The feet hadn't moved at all. Myself and my partner were just fixated on these feet we could see coming from under the door. They didn't move for an even longer amount of time. Eventually me and my partner looked at each other out of fear, turned to again face the door and

nothing. The feet had gone. No noise... Nothing... just gone. I believe if this was a real person, we would have 100% heard footsteps or a door opening or anything, but it was silent... We heard NOTHING. After a short while I plucked up the courage to open the door and look out, again. Nothing. After this I remember just sitting there in a trance trying to rationalize what we had just witnessed.

The Golden Fleece

Me and my partner had been for a drink in the back-dining room of the fleece mid-afternoon. As we were leaving my partner went to the toilet in the middle corridor. While I was waiting, I was stood reading an article that was on the wall. A moment later my partner walked out the toilet door behind me and just as she left the toilet she violently flinched and asked me "did you hear that?" I was confused and replied heard what? She just nervously laughed and told me to shut up thinking I was joking. After she realized I didn't understand from the confused look on my face. She said she heard an old woman croaky voice in her right ear saying, "Open the door".

I told her I heard nothing as it was just me and her in the corridor at this time. She was clearly very frightened by this event as she had a trance like expression and just stood there aimlessly. Then just wanted to leave ASAP. After we left and she had calmed down a little she said it was just an old female croaky voice instructing her to open the door next to her in a very direct manor.

There seemed to be a locked door next to the ladies toilet door where she heard this voice, maybe the voice meant this door? Who knows?

From Braden.

Hi Richard,

I'd like to preface this story by explaining that this occurred in 2006 when I was 13, and I was a troublesome teenager to say the least. I was in the height of teenage angst with plenty of unspent energy, and general frustration at the need to conform to the rules laid out by my parents. This is relevant because on this particular night I had been on the telephone with a friend of mine and it was close to midnight, so my Mother did what most Mother's would do and confiscated my phone and scolded me, telling me in no uncertain terms to go to sleep as I had school the next day. I was very upset about this and threw a loud tantrum, slamming my door and making a ruckus.

I remember this vividly because the fact I was so upset leads me to know absolutely that what I experienced next was not a dream, or a figment of my imagination in a half-asleep state despite the fact it was so late. I was still seething from the argument with my Mum and wide awake, finding it hard to fall asleep. My Mum had gone to bed and I was sat up in my bed watching the television waiting for some of my anger to subside so I could sleep. My bedroom was directly above the kitchen in the family home and all of a sudden, I heard the onset of a commotion in the kitchen below me. For all the world it sounded like someone was carelessly washing up; clattering plates together, dumping them haphazardly in the washing-up rack. Then I heard the cupboards opening and closing in quick succession as if someone was frantically looking for something, just as the plates could then be heard being stacked in the cupboards. Cutlery was clashing together noisily and I could hear the thud of the drawers as they were being pulled outwards with no further leeway to move.

The only people in the house were my Mum and I at this time. My only sibling was at boarding school and my Dad had driven her back to school that very day as it was the end of the school holiday. I knew he was staying over locally to the boarding school that night as it was too long a drive to make it back for the night, but because the noises were so real and vivid I convinced myself that the only explanation was that he must have decided to come back home anyway, clearing the kitchen up before coming to bed. I was so perplexed by this as the noise continued that I knew I had to leave the security of my bed and creep to the top of the hallway to look out the front window to see if his car was in the drive way then the puzzle was solved.

So, this is what I did. I plucked up the courage to go to the window to look for my Dad's car which was petrifying, because the upstairs window was in such a position that I knew I was putting myself in plain view of anybody in the kitchen downstairs. Of course my Dad's car wasn't there, and I could see from the landing that it was pitch black downstairs.

I went into my Mum's room, heart leaping from my chest and I prodded her awake. I remember my words as if it was yesterday, "Mum, I'm not playing a prank on you or trying to wind you up because we've had an argument. There is someone in the kitchen downstairs!" Confused and half asleep, she rolled over and squinted at me. "Mum, there really is someone in the house!" She must have been convinced because she jumped out of bed and grabbed a hold of me. "What do we do?!" she said, trembling. "I don't know!"
The noise had stopped by now, but I was sure that the kitchen would be in disarray. We lingered in my Mum's bedroom for what felt like hours although it was probably only seconds. "We're going to have to go downstairs and check." I nodded and tightened my grip of her arm as we very slowly ascended the stairs with great trepidation, our Lakeland terrier following behind us.

And what did we find? Nothing. Not a thing out of place. The cutlery I had heard and the plates I had heard were nowhere to be seen, not least because my Mum confirmed she'd left nothing out after dinner that night and everywhere was tidied before coming to bed.

Now this story would be strange enough, but the following morning as my Mum drove me to school we were recounting the experience from the previous night and unsettlingly we had both heard something as we stood trembling at the top of the stairs. Neither of us had mentioned it at the time, I think we were too scared to; we certainly didn't want to make the already terrifying situation worse. "Jen?" my Mum said, "The weirdest part was the noise I heard at the top of the stairs". "Don't tell me," I stopped her. "The breathing?" "Yes!" she said.

She confirmed what I had heard. A deep, very deep vibrating exhale from the bottom of the stairs in front of the kitchen door. Even stranger was the fact that our Lakeland terrier Harry had not responded to this event at all, and he was the first to wake at any noise and to bark at any shadow usually.

To this day we have no idea what happened that night, and what we both heard. Was it a poltergeist? I've read many times that poltergeists can be summoned, or rather encouraged, by young teenage girls; their energy and brain activity as they navigate pubescence potentially creating a vortex or a channel for other-worldly phenomenon, and I certainly was a very disgruntled and confused little person at that time!

The house was a new-build and my parents had bought the lot a few years before I was born and seen it built. As far as they knew the land had no historical connections.

From Jenny Hutchings

Hi Richard

Hope you are well? My names Steve from U.K. Ghost Hunting, I have attached a short story below. Along with it is a picture of what we think is a Victorian girl, it's a zoomed picture.

Steve Smith
UK Ghost Hunting

The beginning

I thought I would briefly start at the beginning, to paint a picture, unlike some I was never into the paranormal as a child, in-fact it scared me even to think of it! I had seen some strange ghostly figures as a child but always put it to the back of my mind!

It wasn't until the teenage years I had my first real experience, I was asleep in bed and woke up around 3am, the photos on my bedside wall seemed to have a glow which at first I thought was my DVD player left on and reflecting, as I turned I saw a ball of light the size of a cricket ball come through my wall from my parents room and travelled whilst growing to the end of my bed.

The glow was a white I can't even explain like a "perfect white" it grew into a big egg shape and a lady with long hair stood and smiled at me! I looked at my arms and my hair was on end and I had goose bumps, although inside I felt rather calm. As she disappeared, I felt uneasy and jumped under the covers! In the morning I told my mum, she confirmed to me she also saw a ball of light go from her room to mine.

Since that moment I wanted to delve into the paranormal more to understand what I had seen, the strangest thing is I can now pick up on spirit energy, like the girl spirit had made me aware of my ability? and since then I have been lucky enough to see a few more in my time as an investigator. This is where my story leads to! One of the strangest cases I have experienced!

The Victorian Schoolgirl

We were called to this mansion house near Andover where some workers there and family members had experienced some strange activity! The basement was said to be extremely haunted; workers wouldn't go down alone, things would move on their own, doors would bang and voices and footsteps where heard!

Not knowing what the property was we decided to setup and start investigating. As usual we would do a walk around first and take a few photos where our cctv cameras would go along with our static trigger objects.

The basement really was eerie like a slightly derelict Downton Abbey. We started in the wine cellar with an EVP voice recorder in the center of the room and us sat around a table. We asked questions to see if anyone would come forward! We heard faint footsteps from the corridor followed by the door to the cellar slamming, yet nobody was there!

We listened back and thought we heard a little girl replying, followed by a horrid cackling sound you could associate with that of a witch?

The night carried on being fairly active with high fluctuations of EMF in the old kitchen room, but it wasn't until I got home and scanned through all the photos. Looking through the window from the garden seemed to be a figure, like a little Victorian girl, I had to check the following day if there were any statues in the garden peering in, however there wasn't! On zooming in and playing with contrast etc. I could see a Victorian girl with a bow in her hair and a slightly distorted face! Or was this just Paranoia playing its wicked game with my mind?

I had to know more! Was this girl wanting to tell us a message? I researched the property more and found out it was once a Victorian all-girls school that had to be shut down abruptly due to some of the teachers treating pupils poorly.

Was she there looking for support or to tell us a message? One day I hope to return and find out for sure!

S. Smith

Hi Richard, this happened to me at Carnfield Hall and seems farfetched, but I swear this actually occurred! I was at a paranormal event with Haunted Happenings event company at the time!

"I WAS the footsteps on the stair...." A physical encounter at Derbyshire's most haunted!
I came to be on a paranormal investigation night at Carnfield Hall, near Alfreton in the guidance of a well-established event company. It was your usual put into groups, do calling out, séance Ouija board stuff that every paranormal night involved. Starting off with a guided tour of the place, the haunted bedroom, and the tale of the murdered Squire, either by his disgruntled valet or a burglar, no one seemed sure. Strange thing is that room seemed fine, it was the smaller bedroom at the top of the stone staircase that had a feeling about it. Several of the

more sensitive ladies on the tour were getting palpitations and reported a hint of nausea in there. It was atmospheric and a few of us stated that that was going to be the room we would return to during the hour-long period of release to do your own thing...!

Well the night went well. There were remarkable sessions of spirit communication in the drawing room with some unexplainable knocks and raps emanating from within the floorboards! (We were informed this might be the ghost children who are often seen out playing on the lawns). Many people were getting the walking through cobweb feelings that may be attributed to the touch of a spirit energy. I myself actually felt my balding head stroked at one stage by a gentle, disembodied hand, very peculiar at the time (though it has gratefully happened on a few occasions after that night)!
So, we were all pretty much buzzing when midnight came around and everybody on the event dispersed to whichever corner of the Hall they fancied. I should tell you I was on my solitary own. More than often am when on these nights out. So slightly distracted whilst sat in the kitchen, scrolling through my time lines on the phone, I looked up and found myself entirely alone in there, gulped a mouthful of coffee and headed up towards that atmospheric bedroom where I assumed the majority of them had probably gone, except they weren't.

As I tentatively entered the pitch-black room and shone my torch around there wasn't a living soul in there! The room was decently sized, though the big old four poster bed set against the back wall and old wooden closets and chests of drawers fairly filled the room and leant to quite a claustrophobic feel.

Realising my luck, I thought I should attempt an e.v.p. session before anyone else came in to contaminate, so excitedly turning on the little digital recorder, borrowed off the event company, I closed the door, turned off the torch, and stood in darkness asking out those inane questions we always seem to fall back on. "Is there anybody here?" "Can you tell me your name?" "What date do you think it is?"

All the while the room seemed to be turning darker, was growing slightly oppressive, my eyes didn't seem to be adjusting to the dimness but I just knew there was someone stood at the opposite corner of the room, scowling at me. Though there was nothing to be seen. I played the recorder back, no reply to any of my questions, though my sense of anxiety was going through the roof and the nerves were kicking in. This was unusual for me, I didn't fear anything. I was determined to fight my flight response and tried again for that elusive voice recording from the passed! "This is your chance to tell me your story."

All of a sudden I was overwhelmed by a wave of pent up rage, directed from the something in the corner, my knees buckled, I apologised for disturbing them and I opened the bedroom door, backed cautiously out of the room, gibbering "Thanks for your patience."

Once out on the landing, a bead of cold sweat on my brow, I turned the recorder off and took a step down the stone staircase. Immediately, there was an incredibly loud *STOMP* behind me, I spun about, expecting to see someone petulantly stamping their foot, nothing! I was alone. realising I needed to get down to re-join the event I turned and was enveloped by a cold chill, which grabbed my left shoulder and (I kid you not) the seat of my trousers. And as I tried to maintain my decorum, I was escorted in a frog-marching maneuver all the way down the staircase by that invisible energy. And it didn't release me until I was through the doors at the bottom and out onto the Halls vestibule!

Utterly gob smacked, I rushed into the kitchen where the group were gathered and blurted "You'll never guess what's just happened to me!! ""Have you heard the ghostly footsteps on the stairs?" they ask. "I WAS the footsteps on the stairs!!" I insist. They didn't believe me of course, not at all, in fact they are quite cross that I may have disrupted the energy and ruined the finale of the nights event, where they sit at the foot of the stairs to listen for disembodied foot fall! I know you won't believe me, but it happened to me and has stuck with me ever since as a fantastic encounter with energy and gratitude as well for that frustrated spirits patience, there was some power involved in that interaction and with hindsight it could have done me a bit of damage if it had wanted to and how would I have reacted if some idiot had wandered into my bedroom and bothered me with ridiculous questions whilst I was trying to sleep??

From Chris Willcox

Dear Richard

An experience that myself and a colleague had back in 2015 made several national newspapers after video footage I recorded appeared to show a WWII RAF Pilot standing by the side of a country road. As you can imagine, national newspapers ran their own wording on the story, so I was misquoted somewhat, and of course we were subject to quite a bit of trolling and negative comments.

It was August 2015 and I and colleague Chris Felton were out recording a piece for radio in Otterburn on the anniversary of the famous battle. We both work in local radio, and had visited the location that evening, and we were driving back to Newcastle. The time was around 23:30 and we were driving back on the A696 road, which runs through Northumberland's moors.

Chris was driving and I was in the passenger seat. It had been a long day, so we were quiet and driving back in almost silence. We were approaching the small village of Belsay (Belsay Hall was used in Most Haunted I recall) and the road was still very rural. All of a sudden, I jumped because I saw a person flash past my window on the left. I remember saying to Chris: "You just missed that guy!"

Chris hadn't seen him, but for a few seconds we speculated who it could be - the man was stood at the side of the road and was not fazed by a car driving so close to the verge. He hadn't taken a step back, and just seemed to stare straight ahead. Something didn't feel right. The A696 is a notorious road for fatal accidents, so I joked with Chris that it was a phantom hitchhiker. We turned the car around and went back, and I was recording on my phone. It seemed to last for ages, as we couldn't remember where the exact spot was, but eventually we saw him - still standing there, clear as day. In the video, he is visibly standing there, again, not moving, not flinching, and holding a helmet under his arm.

If you stood at the side of the road, you'd always glance to the side if a car was coming towards you, especially if it was going to miss you by centimeters. This man just stared straight ahead. By now, we were on the other side of the road, so we decided to turn back again so we'd be back on his side of the road. We had the window wound down to see exactly who he was. We were now crawling at about 20mph, but he was gone. No sign of him anywhere. No other cars had gone past so he couldn't have hitched a lift.

If you Google image search the "A696", the first thing you see is an air ambulance attending a serious accident, it's a blackspot. My first reaction was that he was the victim of a fatal road crash. After watching the video back, we paused it, and both agreed he was more like a pilot - he had a uniform on and was holding some kind of helmet under his arm.

I emailed the local newspaper for Newcastle, The Evening Chronicle with the footage. They said they would look into it. That afternoon I received a phone call from a Journalist who said that a historian had uncovered something, and they wanted the exact location of the sighting. I used Google earth and sent them the approximate location. They then told me that the field behind where he was standing belonged to a local farmer, but during the war, it was known as Middlepart Farm. In July 1943, a Spitfire crashed into the fields of this farm during a training mission. To make things even stranger, a Tornado crashed over Belsay in 1999 killing 2 people.

It was in the days following the local news coverage that we contacted by various other journalists. The Mirror, The Daily Mail, The Independent etc. A couple of years later had a Japanese TV station request a Skype interview for a Halloween feature they were doing.

I still don't know what it was I saw - the location was odd for someone to be standing, and he certainly did not seem to be flagging any cars down.

Rob

Hi Richard,

A Primary Encounter! Ghostly headmaster or something worse?

Several years ago, I was working as a relief Caretaker with the County Council, temporarily standing in for staff members who had gone off sick or were on leave. This involved me working in many different schools, old office buildings, public facilities. I didn't realise back in those days, 'how open I was ' to the influence of the 'otherworldly ' had no interest in the paranormal and just accepted as 'weirdly normal' some of the experiences I had previously encountered in quite a few of those properties I'd find myself working in. The incident I am going to relate though changed my life entirely.

The long-time caretaker of this particular village school had retired, his successor had been in post a week when he decided the 'job wasn't for him' and he walked out, leaving the bustling primary school in the lurch!

So, I wound up in this considerably large Victorian period, limestone built Primary School with perhaps early twentieth century extensions. Having to travel a fair few miles to clean and open the school up, I would set off pretty early, reaching the school before dawn most mornings, after a week or so I would notice that there was more often than not, a single light bulb on, in the dark interior of the empty school. There shouldn't have been. I was the one turning all the lights off the night before prior to setting the burglar alarm and locking the doors. Apart from me there was only the headteacher and school secretary with keys, they definitely weren't coming in, they told me. I soon traced the errant light fitting to the long narrow stationery store behind a cavernous classroom, this bulb was activated by movement sensor, someone had to physically walk in to the store to turn the light on, then the light would go off after a few moments of inactivity, so I reported a fault and called the County electrician out to come have a look.

You've guessed it, he couldn't find anything wrong with the sensor at all. He replaced it anyway, because he was 'carrying a spare in the van', but the following morning, there it was, on again, an empty stationery store was illuminated by nobody!

About a week later the schools burglar alarm activated at 3:00 am! First time it had gone off "Ever" apparently!

Now as I've said I lived a lengthy drive away from the school, luckily for me the headteacher, a lovely lady called Jane, lived closer to, (but also a good way out of), the village. So, she had to respond to the alarm companies call out herself! That was fine the first time. But when she started getting the call outs every couple of nights, she started getting a little tetchy with me asking me politely "what the hell I was doing with those alarms??". I should mention that there was never any break in or disturbance within the school property, and I religiously dusted the alarm sensors for cobwebs, loose debris and all, in hope of giving her an undisturbed night. Once again engineers were called out to check and replace any faulty sensors, once again they were at a loss to pin point any problems, they went through the entire system, changed a few, adjusted the sensitivity levels of others, and a night or so after, much to Jane's chagrin, the alarms set off once more, bang on 3:00 am!

All of a sudden, these anomalies stopped! The alarms behaved themselves and desisted setting off, the stationery store light remained off when nobody was in, all was good with the school, the pupils and all the teaching staff were lovely and I had become besotted with the place, spending more time there than I had to and having been there a good nine months or so by now, I seriously considered applying for the full time caretaking position, which for some unknown reason or other the school board of governors hadn't yet rushed to refill!

It was an early summers night, warm and bright, around 6:00pm and there was only me, blitzing through the usual cleaning tasks, Jane the headteacher was sat working late in her office at the opposite end of the building, now this being a typical Council primary school the heating system was still ticking over unnecessarily and as I was just thinking 'how unpleasantly warm the school was', whilst hoovering the carpet of the largest classroom, the room with the stationery store behind, I could suddenly see my breath condensing in front of me, the whole room had dropped to freezing in an instant and felt palpably out of kilter. Shivering uncontrollably my attention was drawn to the far corner of the capacious room, toward the doorway to the stationery store, which now seemed to be filled entirely with a cloud of static energy, just like the static interference you used to get on the old television sets. Before my eyes the energy mass "morphed " into something like a big, big 'man', massively wide, massively tall, dressed in a tweedy jacket. As I stood trying to comprehend what I was looking at, the thing 'launched' itself toward me, running at me with its arms swinging like an old-fashioned rugby forward!!

I had time to wonder "how something so big could move so incredibly fast " when it literally ran straight across the front of me and its travel turned into slow motion, its movements were still impressionistic of someone rushing full pelt, and as it lumbered by I realised it was a man, definitely wearing, tweed jacket and coarse tweedy trousers, though he had no face, nor recognisable head, he was wearing a mortarboard hat and as the now slowly moving bulk continued closely past I could tell he had a gown on his back, which was flapping behind him (as a result of the 'speed' he was running at I assumed)!

In an instant the entity was gone, and I heard the hoover still whirring away full blast, I hadn't noticed any sound at all during those few strange moments I realised! I was left alone in the classroom, wondering what the heck had just happened. I went up into the headteachers office and all I could say was "Jane you never told me there was a ghost here! " "Ghost!" she blustered. "I've been here ten years and I've never seen a ghost"!! I think she was disappointed by that fact, but she did admit next day that I had shook her up quite a lot as my face had the pallor of ashen white!! I certainly was a nervous wreck for days afterwards and I felt physically sick that night when I got home. I would have been drained of all energy of course (I now know). Took a whole heap of courage for me to go back in next morning and open the school up again. But I did, and for a week or so I was fine but jittery. I had to tell my department manager that

I didn't fancy being in there on my own anymore. "Exactly what classroom was it?" he asked, when I described the location he told me matter of factly that " a couple of years ago we had to shut that classroom down, the floorboards had gone rotten and needed replacing. Whilst we were ripping them up we found several old accoutrements from the Victorian school days down in the underfloor space, slate boards, sewing samplers, an old blackboard rubber, oh and that stationery store room, that was the original Head Masters study back in the Victorian day!

So regretfully leaving the lovely, but obviously haunted school in the capable hands of a new caretaker, I resumed my mobile cleaner duties, the ghostly encounter still forefront in my mostly waking thoughts though.

Fast forward several weeks and we are at the end of that same summer and I am doing a litter pick around a small Council cemetery in the Peak District.

As I'm walking between the headstones, I catch a glimpse of a shadowy figure in my peripheral vision, it swoops past incredibly fast, and as I turn to glance toward it this silhouette of a naked, androgynous human sized shape has 'zipped over' into my opposite periphery. I sense this is a man, weirdly made up of a static electrical mass, just like the school apparition had been. There was something not right about this one though, it was full of malice and it began to swoop nearer and nearer toward me, allowing me to see it only from out of the corner of my eyes. When I was much younger, I had accidentally stumbled onto an Arctic Terns nesting ground at Selsey Bill. The ferocious little birds flew down at you to scare you away from their chicks, swishing ever closer on each attack until they are actually tufting your hair with their little talons. I fled from the beach that day beaten by nature and I gathered up my litter picking equipment and fled in fear from the cemetery, beaten by supernatural!!

So frightened had I been by that bone yard guardian I avoided the area for almost a year. It was a warm balmy day when I mustered enough courage and curiosity to go back, butterflies fluttered in my stomach as I approached the gates, and was confronted by a solid, frigid cold invisible force blocking my way. I didn't even push my luck, just waved "good day" at the unseen energy and walked nonchalantly past!

So, was this shadow person connected with the ghostly Headmaster? Had my brush with the school phantom opened my mind to what is normally hidden by the veil? The two incidents certainly led me down the path to paranormal fascination that was definite. Oh, and I finally did get back into the quiet little cemetery, in fact I've been back several times since and never seen the shadow figure again.

From Chris Willcox

Dear Richard,

My name is Andy Woolley and I have a few ghostly tales of my own to share with you, but I do feel a little awkward, only because it is a subject I tend not to mention to most, and as daft as it may seem, I feel a little bit silly.

The first involved my grans apparition, one night, when I was about 6 or 7, and to this day, it still chills me. It has embedded itself forever upon my memory and I recollect it in great detail.

The second involved my sister and I smelling an overpowering scent of roses in our upstairs bedroom when we both were young, say about 9 or 10. We both remember being inexplicably terrified prior to the smell for no reason.

The third involved myself and my pet cat, one Saturday lunchtime. I would have been 11 or 12. I remember being firstly unnerved for some time, the feeling intensified to the point of me being terrified, for no reason, but it felt as if I were not alone. And it was shortly at that apex of fear that the cat tray went wild. I have had an experience of a cat walking upon my back at night, long after the cat had died, even my mate and I experienced an unusual occurrence at Annesley Hall when we explored its ruins during the early 2000's one Sunday lunchtime. We were behind a gutted building, which only displayed the walls of rooms, but no floors longer existed. We both distinctly heard a man's friendly voice, muffled as if from behind a door, coming from above us calling out a friendly, "Hello!?" And we then heard muffled footsteps fall from above, as if upon a carpet.

From Andy Woolley

Hi Richard
I am sending you a story; I hope that's okay! I think I might have said that we live in a peculiar house which is in the Medieval part of the town and as far as I can make from local records, is built on the site of the old asylum. In later years it became a hospital and was then used for teaching domestic skills to young girls who would then be sent out to work as maids and the like in some of the bigger houses owned by the gentry.

The Child
I had fallen asleep in front of the television whilst watching something of very little interest and had woken with a start. I glanced at the clock only to discover it was almost 2am. My wife at that time worked somewhat strange hours, 7pm to 3am. More often than not I would be in bed by the time she arrived home and, sometimes, I might stay up watching a film and would therefore have a cup of tea waiting for her when she got in; this was one such occasion. Deciding to go into the kitchen and wash the dishes from teatime, which should have been done long before now, I first made myself a cup of coffee. This I put on the window ledge above the sink before filling the bowel with water and commenced

with the chore in hand, arranging everything on the draining board as usual. I mention all this purely to demonstrate that I was, by now, fully awake and not in some sleepy trance.

I was now more than halfway through the washing up when, from the corner of my eye I became aware of a presence, in the dining room, someone was watching me! Naturally I thought it to be our youngest daughter, perhaps come down for a drink or to ask if mum was home yet; although I knew this to be unlikely for it was not in her nature to get out of bed in the middle of the night, she would normally call out instead. It certainly would not have been our eldest daughter because she would have spoken as soon as she entered the dining room. Our son, the eldest of all would also have spoken as soon as he came down. That is how I considered it to be our youngest. I also considered that if it was her, she might well be sleepwalking and, with that thought in mind decided neither to make immediate eye contact nor to address her by name. Slowly now I turned towards her and it was then that I realised the figure, which stood no more than five or six feet to my left, was indeed not one of our children.

There before me I saw the image of a child, a girl, not more than eight years old. Because I had directed my gaze to the floor to avoid eye contact should it have been our daughter, I noticed the girl was bare footed and the dress, a pinafore style came to just above her ankles. I am also sure the dress hung from bare shoulders and flanked by what I can only describe as corkscrew type curls but I cannot be positive about this because when I looked upon her face, no discernible details could be seen which threw me to say the least. Where the face should have been there was nothing, it was just grey, almost as if it might be covered in a mist. If perhaps given a little more time, some detail may have become visible, however, that was about as much as I saw because the image just disappeared, nothing dramatic, it was just no longer there! For a moment I felt cold, so cold in fact that it was as though the door to the garden had been flung open and the night air had rushed in. Strangely enough though, I felt no fear, for one thing, it had all happened so fast!

Pulling myself together I immediately went upstairs to check that all was well with the kids but there was no sign that anyone had left their rooms and pushing open the door to the girl's room I could see that they were both still fast asleep. Satisfied that all was well I returned to kitchen and finished the washing-up. I decided not to mention anything to my wife when she got home but waited until the morning. This has not happened again since.

From Ron Smith

Hi Richard,

My experience first starts in November 2014 whilst my parents were visiting from Australia. We were staying at "Edith's House" in Sennen Cove for the week so were doing all the tourist things including a visit to Bodmin Jail.

We had the jail to ourselves, not surprisingly as it was cold! I got separated from my parents at the time as I was following my then 3-year-old son about. We found ourselves in the "long room" and a sense of uneasiness crept over me. As I looked up, I swore I saw a black shadow leap from left to right down the end of the jail. I didn't inspect closer and promptly left the room.

Fast forward to March 2015, my best friend came out to stay with us from Australia. She had booked accommodation at the Jamaica Inn, at the time of booking we had no idea that it also included two nights ghost hunting. It was only when we arrived at the Inn that we found out this also included a ghost investigation at Bodmin Jail, which was only a short drive away. The Bodmin Jail investigation was planned for the first night, the second night was an investigation at the Jamaica Inn. Upon arriving at the jail, Mark Rablin gave us a tour, we then helped set up a few experiments, then started the investigation in the long room. I immediately felt like I had run a marathon race, my heart-rate sky-rocketed and it felt as though something 'rushed' at me. The various REM-pods that were set up were going completely bonkers. A "psychic" who was with the group (I can't remember the group's name, but they regularly investigated with Karin & Colin who headed the Jamaica Inn Team) said that he felt a "new" spirit. My friend, whispered to me, "he wants to talk to you. I keep hearing your name". I had to leave the room; I just couldn't cope with what I could only describe as an intense energy.

That night whilst we drove back to the Inn, I felt an energy in the backseat of the car, I said nothing. My friend jumped in a shower and threw her EMF detector on the bed. I could "feel" the same energy in the room, I picked up the EMF detector and it was going bonkers - could it had been old wiring? I just don't know, but it hadn't done it earlier when my friend was testing it.

Nothing else eventful happened. We arrived back in Hertfordshire and life returned to normal until early one morning I awoke sitting up in bed, I was speaking a different language and a man faded before my eyes. He was standing beside my bed, talking to me. He was dressed in what I would describe as a "great-coat" in was dark Grey and black hair tied back and I felt as though I "knew" him, there was a sense of familiarity. Like a family. I can't describe the feeling, but it felt as though he knew me to be someone else, if that makes any sense? I wrote everything down and researched what I could based on what I saw. The language sounded like old Cornish and I could date the clothing to 18th Century. So, everything fitted.

I had become quite close friends with the team at Jamaica Inn and had joined several of their private investigations. For Halloween 2015 we were investigating Torre Abbey in Torquay, so we had booked a lovely little Airbnb in Devon, just down from The Journey's End Inn. I got home from the investigation in the early hours of the morning and fell into a deep sleep quite quickly which was unusual in itself (I'm a very light sleeper). I had a very vivid dream, I found myself at Bodmin Jail and saw quite clearly (walking down towards the Naval wing) two white crosses appear. The writing on one of the crosses floated up so I could see the name; James Elliott 1787. Then I heard very clearly "FIND MARK. Where's Mark".

Initially I thought nothing of it, but it continuously crept into my thoughts. So, I sat down and did a quick google search of the name, I was pretty shocked to find details about a James Elliott who was executed at Bodmin Jail in 1787 for Highway Robbery. I thought this was a strange coincidence, so I thought I'd email Mark Rablin to validate the information as he was the caretaker and historian at the Jail and had been for many years. (You just can never trust Dr. Google)!

I didn't hear from Mark for some time, turned out he had had a stroke so had been absent. This was well before the Jail took off with its Ghost Nights and Psychic Events, so it was really only Mark who was looking after the Jail and running the events. He confirmed that a James Elliott had indeed been held at the Jail and executed in 1787, he also confirmed that he would have been held in the LONG ROOM but couldn't confirm which cell although he assumed it would have been one of the cells at the end.

I have many stories, but that is one that has definitely stuck with me over the years.

From Laura

Dear Richard,

Tis a short one. Not sure if classified as a ghost but certainly an echo.

My husband and I were on holiday in Cardiff City. We decided to visit Cardiff Castle. We went in and they let you walk the tunnels where they housed people for the bombing during WW2. About a third if the way in, I started hearing children crying and an occasional "there, there love". It was a bit too emotionally charged for me and my husband sensed I was having issues and walked me faster through the ramparts. Near the end, I could still hear people all around, crowded and huddled together. To this day I am still moved to tears from this experience.

From Elizabeth

Dear Richard,

My mum died in 2003 at 2.30 am in January. It was really weird because 30 seconds after she died a black cat walked into the flat. The cat came in from the back door then down the passage to the bedroom where my mum was laid. The cat came into the bedroom sat down and looked at my mum for about 30 seconds, then got up and went out of the flat the same way it came in. All the family where there and witnessed this rather strange event. We had never seen this cat before in our neighborhood and have never seen it again.

Also we had a heart shaped candle burning at the side of mums bed her bedroom window was closed and as she took her last breath the candle went out. Our flat is always well heated but often when I go into mum's bedroom there is an icy chill to the room. I believe mum is still around. I have heard that cats and dogs can detect when someone is going to die. In nursing homes they have been known to go and sit by the bed of someone that's going to die for hours before they died.

From Alan Beadle

Dear Richard,

I would like to share a ghost story from my childhood, which is the event that got me thinking about the whole paranormal subject. Also, I would like to share one from my time in the RAF, and thirdly, an event that happened while in the RAF which was very strange and could be attributed to paranormal. I am unsure that the RAF stories would be suitable for inclusion in a book; however, I hope you find them interesting. A bit about me, I am Jenny, age 44 and live in Lincolnshire, I have been going on ghostly events for about 6 years usually with TPE, although I have had a bit of a break lately due to my mum having Leukaemia and I am caring for her. I grew up in Gloucestershire, and joined the RAF working in Air Traffic Control when I was 18. I was in the Air Force for 9 years but left due to injury and other health problems. I now run a small craft business from home and have been married to my husband Chris for 23 years.

STORY 1

Firstly, my childhood happenings. I was born in Windsor, but when I was 2 my parents moved to Stroud, Glos. I was about 5 when we upsized into an old three-story house which I believe was built somewhere around the late 1800's or early 1900's. It was a row of houses that were all the same alongside a stony road that ended at bollards and a waste ground beyond. I had great fun playing in this area as we were in the second to end house, at the quietest end of the road, and hardly any traffic came along. I could ride my bike up and down without my parents worrying, and the small woods just off from the waste ground meant I could make dens and climb trees to my heart's content. I was a real tom boy and I still have great memories of living there.

The house itself was quite typical for ones built at that time, it had a lounge, small kitchen, small dining room, an underground coal bunker, on the first floor up the stairs were two bedrooms, then some rickety wooden stairs went up past the room that was mine up to the attic where there was one more bedroom and through that was a room that was made into a playroom for me. Strangely I didn't notice anything odd happen in the house until I was around 7 years old. The only thing up until then, was that while playing in the attic playroom, I sometimes felt I was being watched, or that I wasn't alone, it un-nerved me and did cause me to not use the play room very much, but my young brain didn't really read too much into it and I wasn't actually scared of the attic, I still went up there, just not that often.

One night when I was around 7, I had been put to bed and was read a bedtime story, my parents were very strict about bedtimes, I was supposed to go right off to sleep after my story, and wasn't allowed out of bed again unless I needed to use the bathroom. I would never be ready for sleep right away though, so I would usually put my bedside light on and read for a bit. I was sat reading one night when I heard footsteps walk across the landing outside my room. Now I must explain, if one of my parents came up, which they rarely did until their bedtime, I would call out "who is there" And they would say "It's me, go back to sleep". So, on hearing these footsteps, I called out "Who is there" and expected to hear mum or dad answer, but no one answered. So, I called out more loudly, "who is there!" Still no answer. Then I heard the attic door open and footsteps started climbing the stairs to the attic. I was puzzled, firstly, mum and dad had never not answered me before, and secondly, they never went in the attic at night.

All of the attic stairs had very loud creaks and squeaks, and I could hear every one of them making all the creaks they usually do when someone walks up them, the footsteps got to the top and then it went quiet. I sat and waited for the footsteps to come back down but they didn't, and overcome with curiosity, I got out of bed to go and look for myself. If I leaned out from my bedroom door, the attic door was to the left, almost within touching distance, and the stairs wound up round my room. I peered out of my door, and my first surprise was that the attic door was shut and the latch down, I had heard it open but not close, so this surprised me. I walked over to it and opened the door expecting to see the light on, but the light was not on, all I was met with was a pitch black well of darkness and complete silence. I remember feeling the first prick of fear at this point, up until then I had been sure it was my parents, I then heard my parents talk to each other from downstairs, they were watching TV and were not upstairs at all It hit me that what I heard wasn't one of them going up to the attic and I slammed the door, ran back to my room and jumped into bed. The next morning, I told my mum what happened, she said I must have been dreaming, but I knew I wasn't. Later she told me she said that because she didn't want me to be scared, but I will admit, I would have felt better at the time if I knew she believed me.

About two weeks later I was again sat in my room reading, but was getting tired and put my book down turned off the light and started wriggling down the bed to get comfy, as I did this, someone sat on the end of my bed and I froze. The bed dipped right down at the bottom corner as if someone heavy was on it, I could hear the springs of the mattress creaking as they depressed, and my feet could feel that the mattress in that corner now fell away and was not flat any more. I was at this point terrified and frozen; all I could think of is that I must quickly reach for the light and then it would go away. This is what I did, in one move, I grabbed the bedside light switch and clicked it on, and swung to look at the bottom of my bed, I saw nothing but as the light went on, the bed sprung back up again, it was gone. This event really scared me, but the final thing to happen would turn around my idea of being scared and make me feel better, 7-year olds think in odd ways.

We weren't very well off and I didn't have too many toys, but I had a lovely teddy bear bought for me by my Nan. I loved this teddy and would carry it about and play with it a lot. We had a small fir tree in the back garden that would get dug up at Christmas and taken in and decorated, then planted back in the garden every year. I was fond of that tree and would often sit my toys in it. One day I sat teddy in the branches and forgot about him. It rained all night and next day I was looking for teddy when I suddenly remembered he was out in the tree!

 I was so upset that he might be soaked and ruined and ran out to find him, my heart sank lower when I saw the branches of the tree all soaked from rain. When I got to teddy, I was astonished to find him dry! I lifted him off the branch and saw that the branch he was sat on was wet underneath him, and all around him was very wet, but he didn't have a single drop of water on him. I remember deciding that it must have been the ghost who kept him dry and that it must be a child friendly ghost! So, from that day on I wasn't afraid anymore, nothing else ever happened in that house and we moved out when I was 10. When I look back on this, I feel that the attic and bed incidents were paranormal, the teddy may have been a fluke that it was covered by the branches enough not to get wet that night, but I am glad that happened as it took away my fear of being in that house.

STORY 2

My second ghostly story happened years later in the early 90's when I had joined the RAF. I was posted to RAF Valley in North Wales, and actually quite a few odd things happened to me here including dreaming about an aircraft crash 6 months before it happened, also someone who worked in the room at the base of the Air Traffic Tower apologised to me for leaving his post an hour before he should have due to a pen being handed to him by a ghost when he was working alone late at night. This caused him to leap up and run out, going home early. Also, little pet rats I had at the time watching something walk around the room of the block I lived in, and a few other things.

The one I would like to tell you about happened in the med centre at RAF Valley.

Aside from our jobs, we had other duties as well, sometimes weekend duties and other times weekly duties that went to a different person each week meaning that they didn't come round too often as they were shared out between everyone. One of the duties for female personnel was night-time med centre duty. This meant that if there was a female nurse on her own covering the med centre at night and a male patient was taken in, then another female would have to go and spend the night at the med centre that night as well. This is what happened to me, I was on duty for the med centre when I was called and told I would have to spend the night there, I had to be at work at 7am the next morning, so I would stay until 6am then go to work. I arrived at the med centre and was met by the nurse, although a lot of us on the camp all knew each other, I didn't happen to know this particular nurse and so after a quick hello, she showed me to where I would be sleeping. I wasn't really sure what to expect, in my mind I thought perhaps I would be sleeping in some kind of small side room with just a bed in, but she showed me to a long ward with around 5 or 6 beds in a row and said I could sleep in any bed I liked.

I chose the bed opposite the double doors because they were wooden swing doors that had quite large windows in them letting in the light from the hallway. I figured if I woke up disoriented and needed the bathroom, I would have a little light to see by. The nurse left to go to her quarters somewhere down the corridor and I didn't see her again. Since it was already about 11pm I got into bed and settled down. After a short time, I heard footsteps come down the corridor. I thought it might be the nurse coming back and looked up at the doors expecting to see her through the window, I didn't see anyone. The footsteps turned and receded, so I lay back down again. A little while later they came back up the corridor, then turned and kept walking up and down, I was starting to wonder what the heck was going on, why would anyone need to keep walking up and down like that for seemingly no reason.

After a while the footsteps clacked right up to the double doors and paused, I was looking at the doors and saw no one through the windows, I think it was around this point that I realised it wasn't the nurse or any other human doing this and I was none too happy about it. I lay there hoping they would stop, but then the footsteps came right up to the doors again and this time there was a loud banging on the doors, then they turned and walked away. I was staring at the doors for quite some time as the footsteps went back and forth and the doors were banged on. Sometimes the doors shuddered or moved a bit when the bangs happened, other times they didn't move at all. I think some people might have got up and run away, were they in my situation, but I was more afraid of getting in trouble for leaving my post, so I stayed. I listened to those footsteps and bangs all night long, at one point I put a pillow over my head in the hope of getting some sleep, but I couldn't. At 5.30 am I decided to get dressed and go to work, I was so tired that day! I never had to go to that med centre again, but I now wish I had gone back and found that nurse to ask her about what happened and find out what her experiences were while working there, I will never know, but I was glad I didn't have to spend the night there again.

STORY 3

This last story is just a very strange situation that you may find interesting. Do you remember the Peter Moore murders back in the 1990's? I was posted at RAF Valley while this was happening. Peter Moore owned the cinema in Holyhead, which was nicknamed the flea pit, myself and Chris who would later become my husband, did attend the cinema during the time of the murders while it was still owned by Peter, none the wiser that it was he who was the murderer. One of the men he killed was a security guard on a building site (Keith Randles) and this is where my very strange day came in. Just down from RAF Valley is a very small relief airfield called RAF Mona.

It was at the time manned by a small crew of 3 people from 6 am until 6 pm and closed on weekends and at night, it has a very short runway and is usually used for practice landings by the fast jet students who will come down, roll along the runway and take off again without landing. It is generally a long and rather boring day at Mona, and I used to make sure I had plenty of reading material to get through the day with. When I had a shift at Mona, I usually arrived just before 6am in the Air traffic rover, would unlock the tower and drive down the runway to unlock the barriers. Then I would go in the tower and open up everything else while the other two crew turned up by 6 and performed their tasks. I had done this many times and never once felt anything odd about Mona.

At the end of November in 1995, I was on my way down to Mona just before 6 am to open up just as I had done many times before. I pulled up outside the tower and strode towards the building keys in hand ready to unlock the door. I was stopped in my tracks by what I can only describe as an overwhelming feeling that something terrible was about to happen or had happened. It was like a wall I had just slammed into, and the air was thick with tension. I remember looking round and creeping forward a few steps, uncertain and slightly fearful, the feeling that something was badly wrong was intense and I actually felt I was in danger but couldn't understand why. Being fearful of anything was very unlike me at the time, I was very confident back then and generally not afraid of very much, but I did feel afraid at this point. I found myself unable to go any further and went back to my vehicle uncertain what to do. My colleague who was driving the caravan that sits on the end of the runway down to Mona was going to be turning up soon, and would be expecting the tower to be open, I knew he would drive on down the runway, but I wanted him to come with me to the tower so I radioed him and asked him to pull up near my rover.

When he arrived, I was glad to see him but started to feel really silly when trying to explain to him that something just didn't feel right and would he come to the door with me, he agreed but chuckled and we went over to the tower and went in, once we got inside the building the feeling went away and we were able to carry on with our day, but what had happened bothered me a lot. Later my colleague said that outside the tower did have a creepy vibe to it that day, but I had no idea why until I saw the paper the next day. Keith Randles had been stabbed to death by Peter Moore in a building site located not far from the end of Mona's runway on the A5. His body wasn't found until workers turned up for work at around 7.30, so at 6am when I opened Mona his body lay undiscovered. I have often thought, was that feeling I felt that day his spirit trying to alert me to what had happened, or was it just a thick fog of very bad energy hanging in the area from the terrible thing that had happened. I will never know, but I often think about it.

From Jenny Duncan

Hi Richard

I thought I would send this to you as it has intrigued me for a few years now. It happened in Northamptonshire and is a more modern tale.

In 2009 a young (13-year-old) girl by the name of Sophie Bywaters was killed instantly while crossing the A45 dual carriageway one evening having just parted company with a group of friends.

She and her best friend decided to make the risky run across the 4 lanes instead of walking to the nearby overpass. Her friend narrowly made it across but sadly Sophie was hit by an oncoming van and died almost instantaneously.

A couple of years later my sister who is a respected barrister and, totally opposite to me in terms of her lack of belief in the paranormal (her role requires I suppose that she remains rational and pragmatic which is fortunate as she's been like that from the womb) was travelling back in a car with my parents and I after a pleasant trip to London.

We were travelling along the A45 at the spot Sophie died (there are now high fences in place to dissuade others from following her example) and I should point out that the first my sister had EVER heard of the story was right after our tale unfolds as she had been working abroad when the tragedy happened.

She and I were in the back and were immersed in a conversation about the show we had seen when she looked forward at the windscreen suddenly.

She screamed at my Dad who was driving to "Stop Dad, the girl, the girl" and then promptly braced for impact.

It was a horrendous scream, really frightening and my poor Dad swerved and struggled to regain control of the car before pulling over and using words I have never heard my mild mannered Irish gentleman of a father use before, as to why she had screamed and pushed his arm in an attempt to divert the car.

For her part she was utterly bewildered that not only had we not hit anything of substance but that NOBODY else in the car had seen the young girl clearly fleeing across the road.

I should also point out that my parents and sister have never even tried the pleasures of alcohol, (another way in which they differ from yours truly), so her senses and that of my parents were in no way compromised.

I knew of the story of Sophie and told her immediately. At that point, my stoic sister began to shake and cry and was quiet for the duration of the trip.

She's never forgotten it and neither have I and now we know the extent of Dads 'earthy' vocabulary and this was the first time I had known my sister to even acknowledge the question of the existence of the supernatural which I feel lends the account a certain veracity.

She has also mentioned two more occasions of seeing figures by the roadside late at night as she returns from court and me, being a fan of the Fortean world have researched the areas she has mentioned only to find that they are accurate in terms of specific incidents, reported stories and associated dates (one being outside Grace Dieu priory).

I can't tell you how gutted I am that her 'unwanted' psychic prowess seems to sharpen year on year while I am apparently as astute and tuned to the 'world beyond' as a recently squished amoebae and have seen NOTHING of consequence despite devoting 30 years to its study!

From Claire Davy
Hello Mr. Felix. My name is Laura Clarke, and I have many stories from my last home that I lived in for 10 years. My most prominent memory from there is as follows.

It was my son's birthday, and at the time we had ant powder down at all the doorways in the property. My mother was staying with me and my 2 boys at the time. We all got ready for the morning school run, and because of the powder, I made sure the boys didn't go near. Just before we all left the house, I went upstairs to my boy's room and added a little more powder. I made certain to not disturb the powder and we all continued to do the school run. Me and my mother stayed out of the house a good 3 hours, getting my son's birthday things.

We came home, ready to wrap all the presents up for when my son came home, that I remembered that the sticky tape was upstairs. As I approached the top of the stairs, I noticed the ant powder had been disturbed, and immediately shouted for my mother, to which she came up and we couldn't believe what we saw. Large footprints from the powder stopping just a meter away. I know they weren't mine and they definitely weren't there before I left.

From Laura Clarke

Hi Richard, My husband, children and myself lived and ran the Lord Byron Public House Lower Dale Road, Derby. I don't know if I saw a ghost or dreamed it.

I went into labor and had our son at 26 weeks it was a very worrying time as the doctors didn't know if he would pull through but after 17 weeks he was well enough to come home. The night before he was due to come home we set the Moses basket up and got everything ready on my husband's side of the bed as he said he would do the first few nights. Satisfied everything was ready for the following day we all went to bed. In the night I woke looked up to see a man standing at the end of the bed I was so scared I couldn't move to even nudge my husband in bed with me, I couldn't scream or do anything but look at the man, I thought he was going to rob us. He slowly moved around to my husband's side of the bed stopping to look at my husband and then look at the Moses basket, he then looked at me turned and walked through the bedroom wall. I than woke my husband to tell him I'm not sure if I've just seen a ghost or I've had a vivid dream my husband laughed

I described the man in detail my husband stopped laughing and went white. I asked what was wrong he said I had described his dad who I had never met as he died when my husband was seven. A couple of days later we went to visit my husband's mum with our baby who we had named George after my husband's father. When we got there I asked her if she had a photo of her husband and she went upstairs and came down with a battered old photo and sure enough it was the man I had seen in our bedroom.

From Sarah Sargent

Printed in Poland
by Amazon Fulfillment
Poland Sp. z o.o., Wrocław